TRUTH LEFT BEHIND

REVEALING DANGEROUS ERRORS ABOUT THE RAPTURE, THE ANTICHRIST, AND THE MARK OF THE BEAST

STEVE WOHLBERG

Pacific Press® Publishing Association
Nampa, Idaho
Oshawa, Ontario, Canada

Edited by B. Russell Holt
Designed by Dennis Ferree
Cover design (Trade Edition) by Dennis Ferree
Cover design (Specialty Edition) by Gary Will

Published by Pacific Press® Publishing Association
Printed in the United States of America

Unless otherwise credited, all Scripture quotations are from the King James Version of the Bible.

Library of Congress Cataloging-in-Publication Data
Wohlberg, Steve, 1959-
Truth left behind : exposing end-time errors about the Rapture and the Antichrist/Steve Wohlberg.
p. cm.
Includes bibliographical references.
ISBN 0-8163-1846-8 (Trade Edition)
0-8163-1849-2 (Specialty Edition)
1. Rapture (Christian eschatology) 2. Antichrist. 3. LaHaye, Tim F. Left behind. I. Title.

BT887 .W64 2001
236'.9—dc21 2001018542

02 03 04 05 • 6 5 4 3

Contents

Acknowledgments

Truth Left Behind is the result of years of research and the positive influences of many godly Christians. I cannot possibly thank everyone who has contributed to this special project, yet there are a few who most recently stand out in my mind. Leighton Holley for his continual backbone support of my ministry; Costin Jordache and Art Humphrey for their friendship and insights; Pat Jones and Robert Bethel for their assistance with this manuscript; Alan Reinach for his timely suggestions which have been incorporated into these pages; Gary Will for his time and graphic abilities; all my friends at the Texas Media Center; my father, Gene Wohlberg, for his encouragement and constant interest; and my beautiful wife, Kristin, for her love, patience, suggestions, and support during the many hours involved in writing this book.

Above all, I want to thank Jesus Christ, my Savior, who suffered, bled, and died to save me by His grace.

Author's Introduction

On radio, television, the World Wide Web, and in countless other places, Christians are now talking about a best-selling book—*Left Behind*—which is about Bible prophecy, the rise of the Antichrist, and the end of the world. It all began in 1995 when *Left Behind* first hit Christian bookstores nationwide. The authors, Bible scholar Tim LaHaye and writer Jerry Jenkins, scarcely dreamed that Barnes & Noble would eventually call *Left Behind* "one of the top ten best-selling books of the twentieth century." Because of soaring sales and blockbuster success, the authors decided to expand their project into a sequence of twelve books. Amazingly, these books have recently rocketed onto the best-seller lists of the *New York Times, The Wall Street Journal*, and *USA Today*, and have resulted in LaHaye and Jenkins being interviewed on *Larry King Live*. The novels have even been labeled "the most successful Christian fiction series ever" *(Publishers Weekly)*. On February 2, 2001, in the wake of a truly massive advertising campaign, *Left Behind: The Movie* opened in theaters all over the United States.

The primary writer, Jerry Jenkins, is a master storyteller. His *Left Behind* books are fictitious novels which present a fascinating portrayal of what many believe might actually occur during Earth's last days when biblical prophecies described in the book of Revelation are finally fulfilled. The *Left Behind* novels begin with the sudden vanishing of millions of Christians into thin air (an event called the Rapture). The rest of mankind, having been left behind, suddenly wake up to the nightmare of a world gone mad. Driverless cars crash, pilotless planes collide, and universal panic sweeps over the globe as a final apocalyptic period called "the Tribulation" is ushered in. In the midst of unimaginable chaos, the mysterious Nicolae Carpathia, representing the Antichrist, rises to world leadership with promises of peace. Carpathia takes control of the United Nations and quickly establishes a one-world government. Yet not everyone follows this end-time seducer. A group of new Christians, calling themselves the "Tribulation Force," see through Nicolae's disguise and determine to resist his hypnotic power. Finally, in a last-ditch attempt to gain total control of the world, Carpathia unveils his ultimate test of loyalty—the insertion of a high-tech biochip (called the Mark of the Beast) into the foreheads and hands of all people.

Truly, "*Left Behind* is overflowing with suspense, action and adventure" as the video cover of the movie claims. In both the books and the movie, the drama follows the lives of certain people who, having missed the Rapture, are forced to struggle against the Antichrist and his deadly Mark. Just as millions of Americans are now following the lives of their favorite soap opera actors and actresses, even so are millions of Christians now following the fictitious lives of Rayford Steele, Buck Williams, Hattie Durham, Dr. Chaim Rosenzweig, and Nicolae Carpathia as the *Left Behind* saga continues to unfold.

While *Left Behind* is quite imaginative, its hidden power lies in the belief that underneath the fiction lies the rock-bottom fact of Bible truth. Positive comments like this could be multiplied: "*Left Behind: The Movie* is an excellent portrayal of what the Bible declares will actually happen following the rapture" (Dr. Bill Bright, President, Campus Crusade for Christ). "This film is sensitively written, beautifully directed, acted, and produced. I feel it's certainly one of the very best Christian-produced films ever made" (Pat Boone, actor).

Authors LaHaye and Jenkins sincerely hope to impress their readers to choose Jesus Christ immediately so they can go to heaven in the Rapture, escape the Tribulation, and thus avoid having to face the Antichrist and the Mark. There is no doubt that millions of hearts are being touched by this project, that people are being influenced to give their lives to Jesus Christ, and that Christians everywhere are being led to think more seriously about the final days and the coming of the Lord. Even young people are being affected through a special version of *Left Behind* books just for kids, which includes a "Tribulation Force Underground Kit."

Although the producers of *Left Behind* are sincere Christians, nevertheless, I believe it is important to ask the following serious questions: Underneath the excitement of this incredibly popular story, is it possible that something is *just not quite right?* Could it be that in the midst of *Left Behind's* focus on missing people, major Bible truths are also missing? Even worse, could an unimaginable cloud of deception be settling over the Christian world?

The purpose of this book is to take a closer look at what God's Word says about the Rapture, the Antichrist, and the Mark of the Beast. We want to find out whether any significant *Bible truth has been left behind.*

CHAPTER

1

The Rapture—Is Anything Missing?

A Web site advertising the *Left Behind* novels declares: "In one chaotic moment, millions of people around the world suddenly disappear leaving their clothes, wedding rings, eye glasses, and shoes in crumpled piles. Mass confusion hits while vehicles, suddenly unmanned, veer out of control, fires erupt, and hysteria breaks out as the living stare in disbelief and fear at the empty places where their loved ones were just seconds before. This is the rapture that God has planned as the first sign to begin the unraveling of the end of time."

Newspaper headlines are predicted to read: "Millions Mysteriously Vanish!" "All Children Have Disappeared!" "Massive Traffic Snarls Due to Missing Drivers!" "Planes Crash, Trains Wreck as Pilots and Engineers Disappear!" It has been reported that some at American Airlines are worried enough about this to want at least one non-Christian pilot aboard each flight, just in case!

The Bible certainly does teach the exciting truth that Jesus Christ will return for His people. Jesus Himself said, "I will come again, and receive you unto myself" (John 14:3). I fully believe these words and long to be ready for that great day. Without a doubt, the most quoted passage in the Bible now being use to support the idea of a Rapture is 1 Thessalonians 4:17. Countless Christians know it by heart, and it is cited in *Left Behind: The Movie.* Paul wrote that believers in Jesus Christ will someday be "caught up . . . in the clouds to meet the Lord in the air" (1 Thessalonians 4:17). How wonderful! This will be no imaginary, "Beam me up, Scotty," event as in the television series *Star Trek.* On the contrary, it will be very real, and no spacesuits or oxygen masks will be needed. While I do believe in the return of Jesus and that believers will someday be "caught up," there are still some major issues of interpretation that I want to examine. The first concerns *the timing* of our being "caught up," and the second has to do with *the nature* of the event itself.

Let me explain. According to *Left Behind,* the return of Jesus Christ actually takes place in two distinct phases. First, Jesus returns silently and secretly, unnoticed by the world. At that moment Christians will be "caught up," or raptured, which is interpreted as the sudden vanishing of millions of people all over the globe. The rest of mankind, having been left behind, are then ushered into a "seven-year period called the Tribulation" (*The Tribulation Force,* inside front cover). During the Tribulation, the Antichrist arises to enforce his deadly Mark. At the end of the seven years, Jesus returns visibly before the eyes of all, an event referred to as Christ's Second Coming or "glorious appearing." Thus, according to *Left Behind,* Jesus first comes silently to rapture away true believers, and then, seven years later, He comes visibly at the very end of the world. With minor variations, this sequence is now accepted by millions of Bible-believing Christians around the globe as an accurate picture of end-time events.

There are three primary pillars that stand out in this teaching, and it is safe to say that the entire *Left Behind* project rests firmly on top of each of them. They are:

Pillar 1: The Rapture, when the church is "caught up" (1 Thessalonians 4:17), does *not* take place at the visible Second Coming of Jesus Christ, but seven years before it.

Pillar 2: Those who miss the Rapture will have a *second chance* during the seven years of the Tribulation to be saved.

Pillar 3: The true church of today will escape the Tribulation and will not have to face the Antichrist and the Mark.

Before we go any further, allow me to list three logical alternatives, thus clarifying the issues:

Alternative 1: The Rapture, when the church is "caught up" (1 Thessalonians 4:17), *does* take place at the visible Second Coming of Jesus Christ at the end of the world.

Alternative 2: Those who are not ready for the catching up of true believers at the Second Coming of Jesus Christ will have *no second chance* to be saved.

Alternative 3: The church of today will go *through* Earth's final period of the Tribulation and therefore must overcome the Antichrist and the Mark in order to be ready for Christ's Second Coming.

Can you see how serious these issues are? Which view is right—the three pillars of *Left Behind* or these three logical alternatives? *What does the Bible really say?*

Let's start with Pillar 1: The Rapture does not take place at the Second Coming of Jesus Christ. As I have already mentioned, the most widely-quoted passage about the Rapture is found in 1 Thessalonians 4:17. There Paul wrote, "We who are alive and remain shall be caught up." Although the word, "rapture," doesn't appear anywhere in the Bible, the idea comes from those two words, "caught up." A simple comparison of verse 17 with verse 15 ("We which are alive and remain unto the coming of the Lord . . .") makes it very clear that believers will be "caught up" at "the coming of the Lord." Here is the key issue: *At which coming of the Lord will believers be caught up?*

Will believers be caught up at a silent and invisible coming of the Lord before the Tribulation, as taught in *Left Behind*? Or will believers be caught up at the highly visible "Glorious Appearing" of Jesus Christ at the end of the world? Before we read the entire context of 1 Thessalonians 4:17, it is important to realize that Paul uses a very specific Greek word for "coming" in verse 15. The word is *parousia,* and you can find it in any concordance. Actually, a whole lot rides on that one word. If you are a high-tech person, click "Save," and store that word in your mental computer, for we will come back to it.

Have you ever driven down a highway without realizing how fast you were going? Then, when you finally looked down at your speedometer, you said to yourself, "I'm going too fast and must slow down!" This is what we need to do when it comes to our study of 1 Thessalonians 4. We must slow down and take a full look. As we do, we will discover truth that is not only clear, but also shocking. In fact, the implications are nothing short of cataclysmic. Right between verses 15 and 17, Paul wrote, "For the Lord himself shall descend from heaven with a shout, with the voice of the archangel, and with the trump [or trumpet] of God: and the dead in Christ shall rise first" (1 Thessalonians 4:16). *Left Behind* describes this as a silent and secret event, yet doesn't this verse make it seem rather noisy and visible? There is a shout, a voice, and a trumpet. Have you ever heard of a silent trumpet? Some people have even called 1 Thessalonians 4:16 the noisiest verse in the Bible!

Now let's put verses 16 and 17 together: "The Lord himself shall descend from heaven with a shout, with the voice of the archangel, and with the trump of God: and the dead in Christ shall rise first: Then we which are alive and remain shall be caught up together with them in the clouds to meet the Lord in the air: and so shall we ever be with the Lord." Honestly, do you see anything in these words about *vanishing Christians* prior to the Tribulation? Does "caught up" necessarily mean "disappear without a trace"? At the end of His earthly life, Jesus Christ was also "taken up" (Acts 1:9), but this doesn't mean He disappeared, leaving His clothes on earth. Instead, in full view of His wondering disciples, "while they beheld, he was taken up; and a cloud received him out of their sight" (Acts 1:9). Just as Christ's ascension was highly visible, even so do Paul's words—about a shout, a voice, a trumpet, a resurrection, and believers being "caught up" into the clouds—seem to be referring to something quite visible. That is, if we take them literally.

Let's return to 1 Thessalonians 4, and take a look at the entire context:

> For the Lord himself shall descend from heaven with a shout, with the voice of the archangel, and with the trump of God: and the dead in Christ shall rise first: Then we which are alive and remain shall be caught up together with them in the clouds, to meet the Lord in the air: and so shall we ever be with the Lord. Wherefore comfort one another with these words. But of the times and the seasons, brethren, ye have no need that I write unto you. For yourselves know perfectly that the day of the Lord so cometh *as a thief in the night.* For when they shall say, Peace and safety; then sudden destruction cometh upon them, as travail upon a woman with child; and they shall not escape (1 Thessalonians 4:16–5:3, italics supplied).

Paul said this tremendous "day of the Lord" will finally arrive like "a thief in the night." The producers of *Left Behind* interpret this to mean that Jesus will come like a *silent* thief to steal believers out of this world before the seven years of the Tribulation. Then cars will crash, pilotless planes will collide, and babies will be found missing from their cribs. After this, the Antichrist will arise, the Mark of the Beast will come, and people will yet have a second chance to be saved. The popular Christian film, *A Thief in the Night,* which is similar to *Left Behind: The Movie,* also presents this perspective. Yet is this really what Paul is saying?

Again, let's slow down and take a closer look at our biblical speedometer. Paul wrote, "For yourselves know perfectly that the day of the Lord so cometh as a thief in the night. For when they shall say, Peace and safety; then sudden destruction cometh upon them, as travail upon a woman with child; and they shall not escape" (1 Thessalonians 5:2, 3). *Do you see what Paul is really saying?* The fact that Jesus comes as a "thief in the night" does not mean He will come quietly and invisibly to steal believers out of this world, as is taught in *Left Behind.* Rather, it means He will come unexpectedly, bringing "sudden destruction" upon the unsaved. *Thus His coming is not secret, but only sudden.*

What about the unprepared being give a second chance to be saved? Paul clearly answered this question when he wrote, "They shall not escape" (verse 3). Therefore, upon the closest examination, the most widely-quoted text in the Bible—used to support the *Left Behind* idea of a silent return of Jesus, of vanishing Christians, and of people being given a second chance during a subsequent period of tribulation—*doesn't really say this at all!* Paul said Jesus will literally come down from heaven with a noisy shout, a loud voice, and with the blast of a trumpet. This awesome and tremendous "day of the Lord" will come unexpectedly upon all the lost like a thief in the night, resulting in their "sudden destruction."

The apostle Peter also wrote about this same return of Jesus Christ as a thief: "But the day of the Lord will come *as a thief in the night:* in the which the heavens shall pass away with *a great noise,* and the elements shall melt with fervent heat, the earth also and the works that are there in shall be burned up" (2 Peter 3:10, emphasis supplied). According to Peter, the return of Jesus as a thief is definitely not a silent and secret event before any seven-year period of the Tribulation. Rather, this day arrives suddenly, with "a great noise," and is clearly associated with the end of the world! A major crack is starting to form in Pillar 1.

Now let's go back to that mysterious Greek word, *parousia.* There is absolutely no doubt that Paul used this word to describe the coming of Jesus at which believers will be "caught up" (1 Thessalonians 4:17). This same Greek word is also used in a sizzling apocalyptic message given by Jesus Christ Himself in Matthew 24, so we need to take a look at it.

On a certain momentous day, "As [Jesus] sat upon the mount of Olives, the disciples came unto him privately, saying, Tell us, when shall these things be? and what shall be the sign *of thy coming, and of the end of the world?*" (Matthew 24:3, italics supplied). The Greek word in verse 3 for "coming" is *parousia*. The disciples associated this "coming," or *parousia*, with "the end of the world," and they were anxious to know more about it.

Jesus' immediate response was, "Take heed that no man deceive you" (Matthew 24:4). The forcefulness of this thought should hit us like a hurricane! Why? Because it clearly implies that when it comes to this exact topic of the *parousia* of Jesus Christ and the end of the world, there is going to be a great deal of deception whirling around. And even more dramatic is the fact that Jesus actually raised the "Don't be deceived" warning flag *four times* in this single sermon (Matthew 24:4, 5, 11, 24). One gets the idea that last-day delusions would someday sweep over planet Earth like a massive tidal wave. The only way to avoid being swept away in this swirling sea of falsehood is to pay careful attention to the words of Jesus Christ.

Our Lord continued: "For there shall arise false Christs, and false prophets, and shall shew great signs and wonders; insomuch that, if it were possible, they shall deceive the very elect" (Matthew 24:24). Jesus said Satan's delusions would eventually become so subtle and powerful that only "the elect" would come through unscathed. Who are "the elect"? Based on the context, they must be a group of people who know Jesus Christ and the Bible so well that the devil can't mislead them. Verse 31 also tells us that "the elect" are people who are ready for the return of Jesus Christ.

Immediately after warning about tricky false prophets and deception in the last days, Jesus Christ said, "Wherefore if they shall say unto you, Behold, he is in the desert; go not forth: behold, he is in the *secret* chambers; believe it not. For as the lightning cometh out of the east, and shineth even unto the west; so shall also the coming of the Son of man be" (Matthew 24:26, 27, emphasis supplied). Here Jesus draws a razor-sharp contrast between false views of His return and the truth. When it comes to false views, don't miss that little word "secret." Jesus plainly warns that people will mistakenly say that His coming will be in "secret." In fact, based on the context, we discover that this will be one of those powerful delusions, which only God's faithful elect will be able to avoid.

So how should we respond when people say Jesus' coming will be in secret? Christ's answer is stunning. Jesus said, *"Believe it not"!* Why? Because "as the lightning cometh out of the east, and shineth even unto the west; so shall also the coming of the Son of man be."

Far from being a secret event, the return of Jesus Christ will be like the brilliant flashing of millions of lightning bolts blazing across the sky. Can you guess what awesome Greek word Matthew used for "coming" in verse 27? It is *parousia,* and this mega-important word is the exact same word Paul used in 1 Thessalonians 4:15-17 to describe that coming of Jesus at which believers will be raptured or "caught up"! In many Hollywood action films, certain files are labeled "Top Secret," yet when it comes to Bible truth about the "coming," or *parousia* of Jesus Christ, His return will be *anything but secret.* The crack in Pillar 1 is getting bigger.

Paul plainly said that the rapture will take place at the "coming" or *parousia* of Jesus Christ (1 Thessalonians 4:15-17). Jesus Himself said this "coming" or *parousia* will be like the brilliant flashing of electrically charged bolts of lightning hurtling across the sky. The disciples associated this very same awesome "coming" or *parousia* with "the end of the world," and they asked Jesus what the major "sign" of this "coming" would be (Matthew 24:3). After warning about deception and the idea of a "secret" coming, Jesus finally answered the disciples' exact question by lifting the curtain of history and fully unveiling what His high-powered, super-cataclysmic *parousia* will really be like: "And then shall appear the sign of the Son of man in heaven: and then shall all the tribes of the earth mourn, and they shall see the Son of man coming in the clouds of heaven with power and great glory. And he shall send his angels with a great sound of a trumpet, and they shall gather together his elect from the four winds, from one end of heaven to the other" (Matthew 24:30, 31).

This high-impact description of Jesus Christ's return contains an even bigger bang than the highly-speculative Big Bang theory of origins. The "coming" or *parousia* of Jesus Christ, at which believers will be "caught up," will be unmistakably *visible* to "all the tribes of the earth." The amazed masses of mankind will literally "see the Son of man coming in the clouds of heaven with power and great glory." Certainly no one will miss it, and no one will wake up the next day wondering where all the Christians went. On that great day, all of the unsaved will "mourn." Why? Not because their loved ones have vanished into thin air, but because Jesus Christ has *suddenly come,* and they are not ready to meet Him. Once again, this coming will be a very noisy and loud event because it includes the echoing of "a great sound of a trumpet" throughout the sky. When that booming blast is heard, billions of shiny angels will descend and circle the globe to "gather together his elect from the four winds." Thus, true believers will be "caught up" into the air. Now don't miss it. These are the very same elements Paul wrote about in 1 Thessalonians 4:17.

In both Matthew 24:30, 31 and in 1 Thessalonians 4:17, we read about clouds, noise, a trumpet, a gathering together, and believers being transported up into the air. Any concordance will show you that both passages refer to the "coming" or *parousia* of Jesus Christ. In Matthew 24:27, 30, 31, this "coming" or parousia *unmistakably* applies to Christ's "glorious appearing." As we are to be "caught up together," let's put these shocking pieces together. The conclusion is inescapable, unalterable, and irrefutable. True believers will be "caught up" or "raptured" at the loud, climactic, highly-visible, and ultra-glorious Second Coming of Jesus Christ!

This book is like a race car whose engine is just beginning to rev up. We have a lot more to cover, so let's keep going. In Matthew 24, after describing His "glorious appearing," Jesus continued:

> "But of *that day* and hour knoweth no man, no not the angels of heaven, but my Father only. But as the days of Noe were, so shall also the coming of the Son of man be. For as in the days that were before the flood they were eatingand drinking, marrying and giving in marriage, until the day that Noe entered into the ark, And knew not until the flood came, and took them all away; so shall also the coming of the Son of man be. *Then* shall two be in the field; the one shall be taken, and the other left. Two women shall be grinding at the mill; the one shall be taken, and the other left. Watch therefore: for ye know not what hour your Lord doth come. But know this, that if the goodman of the house had known in what watch the thief

> would come, he would have watched, and would not have suffered his house to be broken up. Therefore be ye also ready: for in such an hour as ye think not the Son of man cometh (Matthew 24:36-44, emphasis supplied).

Here Jesus Christ draws a parallel between His return and the sudden descent of billions of tons of water upon the lost in Noah's day. Those ancient people thought Noah was a crazy old man "until the flood came and took them all away; so shall also the coming of the Son of man be" (Matthew 24:39). Can you guess what Greek word is used here again for "coming"? Don't take my word for it, but look it up yourself in your own concordance. It is *parousia,* which, as we have already proven, clearly applies to the visible "glorious appearing" of Jesus Christ.

Now notice, *immediately* after the word *parousia* in verse 39, Jesus continued: "*Then* shall two be in the field; the one shall be taken and the other left" (emphasis supplied). This is probably the second most-quoted text in the Bible now being used to support the *Left Behind* idea of a silent Rapture prior to the Tribulation. Supposedly, when this verse is fulfilled, those who are "taken" will vanish without a trace, leaving only their clothes, shoes, false teeth, and wedding rings, while those who are "left" will have to endure the Tribulation, facing the Antichrist and the

Mark of the Beast. But is this really what Jesus Christ is saying?

The correct answer to this question will not come by depending on the interpretations of others. Actually, it is never safe to lean wholly on any human. Christians should never be taught to rely completely on Tim LaHaye, Jerry Jenkins, or any other popular teacher—including Steve Wohlberg. We all should open our own Bibles, pick up our own concordances, and find out for ourselves what is truth. If you are willing to do this, this is what you will most definitely find: Believers will be "taken" (verse 40) at the "coming" or *parousia* (verse 39), which the Bible clearly applies to the loud, highly-visible, and ultra-glorious Second Coming of Jesus Christ at the end of the world (Matthew 24:3, 27, 30, 31, 39)!

Jesus basically said, "My return will be just like Noah's day" (see verses 37-39). Now think about it. Did Noah and his family vanish before the Flood? No, they walked visibly into the ark. And what about those who were *left behind* after the door of the ark was shut, did they have a second chance? Again, No. How were they left? *They were left dead, they did not escape.* After saying, "the flood came and took them all away," Jesus made His power-packed point: "So shall also the coming [*parousia*] of the Son of man be" (verse 39). And then, without a break, Christ said, "Then shall two be in the field; the one shall be taken, and the other left" (verse 40). Upon careful analysis, these words leave no room for the continuing lives of *Left Behind*'s Rayford Steele and Buck Williams during the Tribulation after the Rapture.

Why not? Because those who are "taken" are taken up at the "coming" or *parousia,* which applies to the visible "glorious appearing" of Jesus Christ!

Immediately after saying, "One shall be taken, and the other left," the King of the universe then compared His Second Coming to the sudden arrival of a midnight thief, just like Paul did in 1 Thessalonians 5:2, 3. Jesus said, "But know this, that if the goodman of the house had known in what watch the thief would come, he would have watched, and would not have suffered his house to be broken up. Therefore be ye also ready: for in such an hour as ye think not the Son of man cometh" (Matthew 24:43, 44). To "watch" doesn't mean spending endless hours in front of the television set, nor does it mean watching popular movies about the end times, which may take detours away from the straight truth. It means to *watch out for deception!*

Matthew 24 and 1 Thessalonians 4 and 5 fit together just as perfectly as Adam and Eve did before they sinned. Both passages describe a noisy, loud, highly-visible, trumpet-blasting, ultra-glorious return of Jesus Christ in the clouds. Both describe believers being caught up and transported into the air. Both declare this day will come with thief-like suddenness upon all sleeping sinners. In Noah's day, when billions of tons of water came crashing down, there were no second chances for those outside the ark. Paul said the lost "shall not escape." And both Paul and Matthew use the exact same Greek word to describe this great, tremendous, and awesomely powerful "day of the Lord." Simply look in your concordance. That word is *parousia,* which clearly refers to the Second Coming of Jesus Christ. True believers are urged to watch, be ready, and to avoid all satanic deceptions.

What about the rapture taking place "in a moment, in the twinkling of an eye" (1 Corinthians 15:52)? This is probably the third most-quoted text in the Bible now being used to support the idea of vanishing Christians prior to the Tribulation. We have previously slowed down to look at our biblical speedometer, yet this time we must come to a screeching halt. Paul wrote, "Behold, I shew you a mystery; We shall not all sleep, but we shall all be changed, In a moment, in the twinkling of an eye, *at the last trump: for the trumpet shall sound,* and the dead shall be raised incorruptible, and we shall be changed" (1 Corinthians 15:51, 52, emphasis supplied). Is Paul saying that believers will mysteriously vanish from the earth prior to the Tribulation, while their loved ones blink? Not at all! He is saying that the dead will be raised and our bodies will be changed "in a moment, in the twinkling of an eye." But *when* will this "moment" take place? Paul's answer is clear; it will occur *"at the last trump,"* when "the trumpet shall sound," at the end of the world. This is that very same "great sound of a trumpet" Jesus said would be heard at His Second Coming (Matthew 24:31)! Pillar 1 is cracking and crumbling.

As we have previously noted, Pillar 2 supporting the *Left Behind* project is the theory that those who miss the Rapture will have a *second chance* to be saved during the Tribulation. *This idea can be dangerous.* Some people might rationalize, "If the Rapture really takes place, then I'll know for sure God is real. It may be tough, but I can still join the "Tribulation Force" during the seven years. Even if that Antichrist guy tries to kill me, I will still resist the Mark of the Beast!"

While the fostering of this foolish attitude is not the intent of the authors of *Left Behind,* people can easily adopt this "wait and see" position, putting off their decision to follow Jesus Christ. But Paul wrote that all who are not fully on the Lord's side when believers are "caught up . . . shall not escape" (1 Thessalonians 4:17; 5:3), and there were no second chances in Noah's day. After the door of the ark closed, all desperate attempts to get inside were useless. Therefore, Pillar 2 is becoming like a man diagnosed with cancer; it has very serious problems.

If Pillars 1 and 2 supporting the *Left Behind* project are wrong, and if the logical alternative about the church being "caught up" at the Second Coming of Jesus Christ is right, then this means that the church of today is destined to go through the Tribulation, rather than disappearing before it arrives. Yet Christians often resist this conclusion with the argument, "God wouldn't allow us to go through the Tribulation because He loves us too much." But think about it. Would He love the "Tribulation Force" after the Rapture any less? Obviously not. Then why would He allow them to go through such a period? Could it be that the doctrine of *escaping tribulation* is really only catering to our middle-class American tendencies? We like comfort and hate to go through trials; we can hardly bear it when our TV-dinner lifestyle is threatened. Yet historically, God's people have gone through intense suffering. All of the disciples of Jesus, except John, were cruelly murdered. Thousands of the early Christians were literally torn to shreds by wild dogs and lions in the Coliseum. Millions of others were horribly tortured by the Inquisition and burned to ashes during the Dark Ages. Believers in Russia and China have suffered terribly under Communism. And yet American Christians say, "God wouldn't allow us go through the Tribulation!"

When it comes to this topic of "tribulation," once again, concordances can come in handy. If you look up the word, "tribulation," in Strong's or Young's concordance, you may be shocked to discover that almost every reference describes *the suffering of believers.* Jesus told His followers: " 'In the world ye shall have *tribulation*' " (John 16:33, emphasis supplied). Paul told his early Christian converts: "We must through much *tribulation* enter the kingdom of God" (Acts 14:22, emphasis supplied). Paul wrote to the church at Thessalonica: "We ourselves boast of you among the churches of God for your patience and faith in all your persecutions and *tribulations* that you endure" (2 Thessalonians 1:4, emphasis supplied). On the lonely Isle of Patmos, John was our "brother and companion in *tribulation*" (Revelation 1:9, emphasis supplied). Jesus told His church in Smyrna: "I know thy works, and *tribulation*" (Revelation 2:9, emphasis supplied). In the light of these scriptures, the idea of Christians escaping tribulation seems like fantasy and illusion.

Some Christians might respond by saying, "Yes, but those verses are talking about 'tribulation,' not '*the* Tribulation.' " But think about it. If the majority of the Bible's "tribulation texts" refer to what believers go through, why would God's Word suddenly shift gears by teaching that "*the* Tribulation" is something believers will *not* go through? Even in *Left Behind,* there are Christians who do go through *the* Tribulation (the "Tribulation Force"), therefore the thought of Christians going through this period is not really so strange.

Many Christians also say, "If the church is going through the Tribulation, then why isn't the church mentioned after Revelation 4?" Let's take a closer look. In Revelation 4:1, John was told to "come up hither." People conclude this represents the Rapture, and they think the church isn't mentioned anymore.

First, John did not actually go to heaven in Revelation 4:1; he was simply taken up *in a vision,* while his toes were still on Patmos. Second, the church *is* on earth after Revelation 4. How do we know this? Because the Bible says the Antichrist will make "war with *the saints*" (Revelation 13:7, emphasis supplied). Then we read about "the faith of the saints" (verse 10), and during the Mark of the Beast crisis, Revelation refers to "the saints" who keep "the faith of Jesus" (Revelation 14:12).

Many might respond by saying, "Yes, but those are the Tribulation saints after the Rapture, not the church." But consider this. Paul wrote his New Testament letters to the "churches of the saints" (1 Corinthians 14:33). What does this tell us? It tells us that wherever there are saints, *there is the church!* Even if the saints mentioned in Revelation 13 and 14 are only the Tribulation saints after the Rapture, wouldn't they, as sincere believers in Jesus Christ, *still be the church?*

Left Behind teaches that the church will not be on earth for Armageddon. Is this true? The word "Armageddon" occurs only one time in the Bible—in Revelation 16:16—which is the great chapter about the falling of the seven last plagues.

Right before verse 16, *during* the time of the seven last plagues, Jesus Christ thunders, " 'Behold, I come as a thief. Blessed is he that watcheth, and keepeth his garments, lest he walk naked, and they see his shame. And he gathered them together into a place called in the Hebrew tongue Armageddon" (Revelation 16:15, 16). Did you catch that? Who is Jesus talking to? To the church! At the time of verse 15, *while* the seven last plagues are falling, and right before the battle of Armageddon, Jesus Christ has not yet come as a thief! Therefore, He must come like a thief *at Armageddon, after* the Tribulation, and this must be the time when He comes to gather His church.

Like a good commanding officer, Paul urged the soldiers of the cross to, "Take unto you the whole armour of God, that ye may be able to withstand in the evil day, and having done all, to stand" (Ephesians 6:13). How can we stand in "the evil day" if we have previously disappeared? Jesus Christ also said, "He that shall endure unto the end, the same shall be saved" (Matthew 24:13). So how long must we endure? *To the end.* Yet Christ will be with us. That is why He promised: "I am with you alway, even unto the end of the world" (Matthew 28:20). We can trust Him in this.

If what *Truth Left Behind* is saying is true, then what about "the seven years"? The concept of a seven-year period of tribulation is actually the underlying foundation of the entire *Left Behind* scenario. Remember, the theory is that first the

Rapture takes place, and then comes the seven years of the Tribulation. One of the popular *Left Behind* novels says, "The disappearances have ushered in a seven-year period of Tribulation" (*The Tribulation Force,* inside front cover). In another we read, "It's the midpoint of the seven-year Tribulation." (*The Indwelling,* inside front cover). Thus, this *New York Times* best-selling series of fiction books now being endorsed by well-respected Christian leaders nationwide, is built completely around this seven-year framework.

The great-granddaddy Bible text for the entire seven-year tribulation theory is Daniel 9:27, which is the very first verse quoted in *Left Behind: The Movie.* This is what the text says: "He shall confirm the covenant with many for one week: and in the midst of the week he shall cause the sacrifice . . . to cease." A day in prophecy represents a literal year (see Numbers 14:34; Ezekiel 4:6). Thus, this famous period of "one week" in the prophecy actually represents seven literal years. Millions are now applying this to a future seven-year period of the Tribulation. "He" is interpreted to be the Antichrist who will make a covenant with the Jews during the Tribulation. Book 6 of the *Left Behind* novels is called, *Assassins.* The subtitle reads: "Assignment: Jerusalem, Target: Antichrist." It's focus is "the half-way point of the Global Community's seven-year protection agreement with Israel" (p. 302).

According to *Left Behind,* immediately after

the Rapture, the Antichrist will make this "seven-year protection agreement with Israel." Yet I wonder how he could accomplish this so quickly right after the Rapture. Wouldn't he need some time to rise to power? An intrinsic part of this story is the theory that, during the Tribulation, the Jewish temple will be rebuilt and animal sacrifices will be resumed (more on this later). Supposedly, half way into the Tribulation, the Antichrist will break his "protection agreement" with the Jews and stop the sacrifices, causing them "to cease." This is how literally millions of Christians today are interpreting Daniel 9:27.

What many don't realize is that there is another reasonable interpretation, which is quite different. Not only does this alternate view have a great deal of biblical support, but it has also been taught in the past by many credible Bible scholars who have written respected commentaries, which are now in the libraries of pastors across America. One example is the world-famous Matthew Henry's *Bible Commentary.* Shockingly, this commentary doesn't apply Daniel 9:27 to the Antichrist at all, nor does it apply the "one week" to a seven-year period of tribulation after the Rapture. Rather, it applies it *to Jesus Christ,* who, after three and a half years of loving ministry, died "in the midst of the week," which ultimately caused all animal sacrifices to cease!

Here's the quotation from Matthew Henry's famous commentary: "By offering himself a sacrifice once and for all he [Jesus] shall put an end to all Levitical sacrifices" (Matthew Henry's *Commentary on the Whole Bible,* Vol. IV, Isaiah to Malachi, Complete Edition. New York: Fleming H. Revell Co. 1712, notes on Daniel 9:27, p. 1095).

Another excellent Bible commentary, written by the well-known British Methodist, Adam Clarke, says, This confirmation of the covenant must take in the ministry of John the Baptist with that of our Lord, comprehending the term of seven years, during the whole of which he might well be said to confirm or ratify the new covenant with mankind" (*The Holy Bible with a Commentary and Critical Notes* by Adam Clarke, Vol. IV, Isaiah to Malachi. New York: Abingdon-Cokesbury Press, notes on Daniel 9:27, p. 602). Here's one more quotation from the much-respected *Jamieson, Fausset and Brown Commentary*: "He shall confirm the covenant—Christ. The confirmation of the covenant is assigned to Him" (Rev. Robert Jamieson, Rev. A. R. Fausset. and Rev. David Brown, *A Commentary Critical and Explanatory on the Whole Bible,* Complete Edition. Hartford, Conn.: S.S. Scranton Co., notes on Daniel 9:27, p. 641). All of these commentaries are now available electronically on the World Wide Web so you can easily check these references yourself.

Which view is right—the one put forth in *Left Behind* or the one described in these dusty old commentaries? Does Daniel 9:27 apply to a future seven-year period of tribulation or was it fulfilled by Jesus Christ 2000 years ago? The only way to find out is by taking a careful look at Daniel 9:27 itself. God's Word says, "He shall confirm the covenant with many." Now take a look at this. Jesus Christ Himself said, " 'This is My blood of the new covenant, which is shed for many' " (Matthew 26:28, NKJV). Behold a perfect fit! Both texts use the words "covenant" and "many." Popular teaching says the Antichrist will make a covenant or "protection agreement" with the Jews and then break it after three and a half years. Yet the Bible actually says, "He shall *confirm* the covenant with many for one week" (emphasis supplied). Thus, "He" is to *confirm* the covenant for the full seven years, not break it! And it is not simply "a covenant," as is commonly understood. No! It is "*the* covenant," which applies to the New Covenant. Our Lord Jesus Christ is the One by whom "the covenant . . . was confirmed" (Galatians 3:17; see also Romans 15:8). In the midst of the week, after three and a half years, Jesus gave His life for us, "[causing] the sacrifice . . . to cease." He was the final sacrifice. No more sacrifices are to be offered (see Hebrews 10:12). Period.

In my earlier book, *Exploding the Israel Deception*, chapter 5 is called, "The Seventieth Week of Daniel Delusion" (see the back of this book for more information). There, I give many more solid reasons why Daniel 9:27 doesn't apply to the Antichrist at all, but to Jesus Christ alone. The fact is, the entire *Left Behind* idea of a seven-year period of tribulation after the Rapture is a grand illusion, a massive mega-myth. It may even go down in history as the greatest evangelical misinterpretation of all time! The whole concept is like a gigantic bubble. Once Daniel 9:27 is correctly understood, and the sharply-pointed pin of truth is inserted—"Pop goes the seven years!"

I want to conclude this chapter by talking about Pillar 3, which now supports the *Left Behind* house—the idea that the church of today will *escape the Tribulation* and will *not* have to face the Antichrist and the Mark of the Beast. This is the big one, and it is right here that emotions fly and reason vanishes just as quickly as those disappearing Christians in *Left Behind: The Movie*. Why? The answer is simple. If Pillar 3 is false, and if the church will not be "caught up" until the Second Coming of Jesus Christ, then this obviously means that the church must *first* pass through Earth's final period of Tribulation and will have to face the Antichrist and the Mark of the Beast. Many Christians fear such a conclusion. And this is why, many times, underneath the attempt to maintain the doctrine of a pre-Tribulation *secret* Rapture, there often lurks a *secret* fear of having to face the Mark of the Beast.

This reminds me of the tragic deaths of 118 crewmen inside the giant Russian nuclear submarine *Kursk*. On Saturday, August 12, 2000, way down in the icy waters of the Barents Sea, something went terribly wrong. An explosion took place, followed by another. The "catastrophe developed at lightning speed" (*Newsweek*, November 6, 2000, p. 42), and the doomed sub quickly sank to the bottom of the ocean. *Newsweek* magazine ran a story called, "A Cry From the Deep," which mentioned a letter that was found by deep-sea divers inside a pocket of one of the corpses. Evidently, twenty-three Russians survived the initial blasts and flooding. The note said: "There are 23 people here. . . . None of us can get to the surface" (Ibid.). Because help didn't come quickly enough, they all died. As I have thought about this, I have tried to imagine the terrible feeling of fear in the hearts of those Russian sailors deep down below the calm surface of the water.

Fear also lurks below the doctrine of a pre-Tribulation rapture. Deep down underneath the surface of many arguments, lies a hidden fear of having to face the Mark of the Beast. This fear may be unconscious, yet often it is there. But it need not be. True Christians can learn a lesson from popular bumper stickers, which say, "Fear No Evil." We don't need to be afraid. We can trust in Jesus Christ, for hasn't He promised, "Lo, I am with you alway, even unto the end of the world" (Matthew 28:20)? If the fictitious "Tribulation Force" in the *Left Behind* novels can overcome the Antichrist and the Mark of the Beast, then *so can we!* Yet Christians *do* fear the Mark, and this fear often prevents them from even reasonably examining the clear scriptural evidence in favor of a post-Tribulation gathering of the church to Christ. And thus, sadly, the pre-Tribulation Rapture idea has become the great evangelical escape clause for the avoidance of the Mark of the Beast! And for those who must have it that way, no amount of biblical evidence will convince them otherwise. Like a triple-bolted door in downtown New York, they are closed to the facts.

The result? *Truth is left behind.*

CHAPTER

2

Jesus Christ and the Antichrist

When most Christians think about the Antichrist, they usually think about one super-sinister individual who will rise into power in Europe after the Rapture. The fictitious Nicolae Carpathia, the Antichrist in the *Left Behind* novels, is a perfect example of such thinking. Carpathia is portrayed as a Romanian, brilliant, an astute politician, a born leader, "one of the most powerful and charismatic personalities ever" (*The Tribulation Force,* ix). He quickly seizes power after the Rapture, takes control of the United Nations, and establishes a one-world government during the Tribulation. Speaking gentle, compassionate words to the masses, he is secretly "indwelt by the devil himself" (*The Mark—The Beast Rules the World,* inside cover). Underneath his warm and winning exterior, lies hidden "the monster within" (Ibid., p. 2). The world openly worships him as God, after he becomes the "Supreme Potentate, His Excellency Nicolae Carpathia" (Ibid., xi).

Because most Christians firmly believe the Antichrist will be a single person like Carpathia, and because millions sense the Rapture is near, some are even now speculating about who this inwardly evil individual might be. In the last few years, some have suggested Prince Charles, others Mikhail Gorbechev, and still others Bill Gates, the founder of Microsoft! One person even went so far as to suggest that the Antichrist might be David Hasselhoff, star of the incredibly popular television series *Baywatch.* The location of the show is the Pacific coast where David plays a lifeguard named Mitch. Because Revelation 13:1 describes the beast as coming out of the sea, David seems to this person to be a perfect fit! Of course hardly anyone has taken this suggestion seriously. But the fact remains, Christians everywhere are definitely expecting someone sinister—a mysterious, evil person—to rise up as the Antichrist.

What does the Bible really say about the Antichrist? The word, "antichrist," or "antichrists," is used only five times in the New Testament, and these are all found in 1 and 2 John. We are about to begin an awesome journey into one of the most misunderstood of all Bible subjects. It is super hot, yet here we go. Almost 2,000 years ago, John wrote, "Little children, it is the last time: and as ye have heard that antichrist shall come, even now are there many antichrists; whereby we know that it is the last time. They went out from us" (1 John 2:18, 19).

Do you realize what this text says? John's points are more explosive than an erupting volcano. Here's a simple summary:

1. The early Christians had heard that antichrist was coming.
2. Even in John's day many antichrists had come.
3. This is evidence that "the last time" has already arrived.
4. These antichrists "went out from us."

This is truth stranger than fiction. When most Christians think about the Antichrist, they think of only one sinister person, like Carpathia, yet John said there are "many antichrists." When most Christians think about the Antichrist coming, they place this development only in the future after the Rapture. Yet John wrote that many antichrists are here "even now." When most Christians think about the Antichrist, they think he will appear only during that "seven-year period called the Tribulation" (*The Tribulation Force,* inside cover). Yet John said "the last time" *is here now!*

When most Christians think about the Antichrist, they think of someone who is blatantly anti-Christian, who will openly make war against a group of post-Rapture people (like the "Tribulation Force"). But John said, "They went out from *us.*" What does this mean? John uses the word "us" in reference to himself and other Christians of the early church. In other words, the antichrists John was describing were rising up from *inside of Christianity!* According to John, many antichrists are already here, the last time has come, and these antichrists have come from *within* the Christian church. Does Nicolae Carpathia pass these biblical tests? Like an "F" on a final exam, he fails *at every point.*

Again John wrote, "Who is a liar but he that denieth that Jesus is the Christ? He is antichrist, that denieth the Father and the Son. . . . These things I have written unto you concerning them that *seduce* you." (1 John 2:22, 26, emphasis supplied). These words are of great importance. The Antichrist will deny the Father and the Son, yet this denial will be *seductive,* not openly obvious. Let's examine this. Jesus said, "I am the way, the truth, and the life: no man cometh unto the Father, but by me" (John 14:6). The Father is God. Jesus, the Son, is the only way to the Father. Paul also wrote, "There is one God, and one mediator between God and men, the man Christ Jesus" (1 Timothy 2:5). Our heavenly Father loves us, that is why He sent Jesus, His only Son. As trusting children, we can come to our heavenly Father directly through Jesus Christ. We don't need any other mediator or go-between, for His loving arms are open wide. And this Mediator is "the man Christ Jesus."

Again John warned, "Every spirit that confesseth not that Jesus Christ is come in the flesh is not of God: and this is that spirit of antichrist, whereof ye have heard that it should come; and even now already is it in the world. Ye are of God, little children, and have overcome them: because greater is he that is in you, than he that is in the world" (1 John 4:3, 4). Thus, the Antichrist will deny that Jesus has come in *"the flesh."* What does His coming in the flesh mean? First, it means that Jesus is fully human. He loves us and understands us completely. Next, because Jesus has come in *the* flesh, He is now " '*the* way, *the* truth, and *the* life' " (John 14:6, emphasis supplied). No one comes to the Father but through Him. He is our only Mediator, *"the* man Christ Jesus" (1 Timothy 2:5). This is why we don't need any other mediators! Yet the Antichrist will deny this, though not obviously, but seductively.

And did John look for this Antichrist only in the future during the Tribulation? No, for he wrote, "Ye have heard that it should come; and even now already is it in the world." According to John, "it" is here now, and "it" *is more than one single person like Nicolae Carpathia.* There is a mysterious "spirit of antichrist." And who is to fight this antichrist spirit? John wrote to Christians, saying, "*Ye* are of God, little children, and have overcome them" (emphasis supplied). Who is to "overcome" these many antichrists? True Christians! The Bible says, "*You!*" Yet this is entirely contrary to the idea in the *Left Behind* books and movie that Christians today will not have to face Antichrist because he comes only after the Rapture! Is something "seductive" going on around here?

What I am about to say may shock you, yet it's entirely true. The current wildly popular idea of a one-man Antichrist like Nicolae Carpathia who comes only after the Rapture is a *new doctrine,* at least when it comes to Protestants. From the 1500s down to the early 1900s, the majority of Baptists, Methodists, Congregationalists, Lutherans, Anglicans, Presbyterians, and Mennonites believed, based on a careful study of Scripture, that the Bible's predictions about "antichrist" (1 John 2 and 4), "the little horn" (Daniel 7), "that man of sin" (2 Thessalonians 2), "the Mother of Harlots" (Revelation 17), and "the beast" (Revelation 13) *all apply most specifically to the Roman Catholic Church. Newsweek* magazine has reported, "Martin Luther was the first to identify the papacy as such with the Antichrist. At first he discounted the value of John's Apocalypse. But then he saw in it a revelation of the Church of Rome as the deceiving Antichrist . . . a view that was to become dogma for all Protestant churches" (*Newsweek*, Nov. 1, 1999, p. 72).

"Wycliffe, Tyndale, Luther, Calvin, and Cranmer; in the seventeenth century, Bunyan, the translators of the King James Bible, and the men who published the Westminster and Baptist Confessions of Faith; Sir Isaac Newton, Wesley, Whitfield, Jonathan Edwards; and more recently, Spurgeon, Bishop J. C. Ryle and Dr. Martyn Lloyd-Jones; these men among countless others, all saw the office of the papacy as the antichrist. . . . The Reformers and their heirs were great scholars and knew the Word of God and the Holy Spirit as a living teacher" (*All Roads Lead to Rome*, Michael de Semlyen. Dorchester House Publications, 1991, pp. 205, 206). If any of these men could have been transported into a twenty-first-century theater showing *Left Behind: The Movie*, they would have wondered, "What is this all about?"

In this little book I am going to talk plainly about Protestants and Catholics. Yet first, I want to make a few things clear. I have no desire to attack individuals on either side. I fully believe that Christians of every denomination will be in the kingdom, and I hope to join them. Catholics are now helping tens of thousands of people through orphanages and in many other ways. People are people, and Jesus Christ deeply loves every one of us, no matter what church we belong to.

As an interested observer of the religious scene, I recognize contemporary Catholicism's diversity, and that millions of American Catholics do not subscribe to all of the doctrines of the Vatican. Yet I am also a student of prophecy who shares the view of the major Protestant Reformers. Like them, I do not apply the words of Daniel, Paul, and Revelation to individual Catholics, but rather *to the papal system as a whole* with its still-current doctrines about heavenly mediators (Mary and the saints), forgiveness only through priests, purgatory, and no salvation outside of the Mother Church.

Jesus Christ is the only way to the Father (John 14:6). There is only one Mediator up there in heaven, and it is "the man Christ Jesus" (1 Timothy 2:5). "Believe on the Lord Jesus Christ, and thou shalt be saved" (Acts 16:31). These are solid Bible facts. Yet historically, and at present, these truths are still officially denied by the Vatican. Catholics are still sincerely, and yet mistakenly, being taught to look to Mary and to many other saints as mediators. To date, the Roman Catholic Church still does not accept the idea that Christians can be saved by faith in Jesus Christ without going through the Church. *Who really is the beast of prophecy?* Will it be someone like Nicolae Carpathia or was Martin Luther correct? Why did the belief that papal Rome was the Antichrist, "the beast," and "the little horn," become "dogma for all Protestant churches" (*Newsweek*, Nov. 1, 1999, p. 72)? It's time to find out by carefully studying the Bible.

Daniel 2 describes four successive kingdoms—Babylon, Persia, Greece, and Rome. There is no question about this anywhere. Daniel 7 also describes four kingdoms, using the symbols of a lion, a bear, a leopard, and a dragon-like beast with ten horns. Daniel 7:23 is a very important text, so don't miss it. It says, "The fourth beast shall be the fourth kingdom upon the earth." So, what does a beast represent in prophecy? Does it represent a single, solitary, devil-indwelt man like Nicolae Carpathia? Or possibly some gigantic 5,000-gigabyte super computer? No. According to Daniel 7:23, *a beast represents a kingdom.* Never forget this! This truth is like a gigantic fork in the road. If we make a mistake here, we might end up thinking Bill Gates is the beast! Daniel 7:23 is truly a foundational text that will save us from global delusions. Based on history and the clear parallels between Daniel 2 and 7, the fourth beast represented the Roman Empire.

It's time to focus on "the little horn" of Daniel 7. Catholics, Protestants, and Evangelicals, including the authors of *Left Behind,* all agree that this horn represents the Antichrist. It is the *interpretations* of this passage that vary. Here are nine fast facts about the little horn in Daniel 7:

1. The little horn comes out of the fourth beast, that is, out of the Roman Empire (Daniel 7:7, 8).
2. It rises "among" the ten horns that di-

vided up that very empire (verse 8).
3. It comes "after" the ten horns are in place (verse 24).
4. It will be "diverse" or different from the other ten horns (verse 24).
5. It will "[pluck] up by the roots" three of the first ten horns (verse 8).
6. It has "eyes like the eyes of a man" (verse 8).
7. It has "a mouth speaking great things" (verse 8).
8. It will wage "war with the saints" (verse 21).
9. It will rule for "a time and times and the dividing of time" (verse 25).

As surely as George Washington was America's first president, even so are these nine points sure facts in Daniel 7.

Most of those talking about the prophecies today apply the "little horn" to someone like Nicolae Carpathia. Most realize the four beasts in Daniel 7 represent Babylon, Persia, Greece, and Rome. But then they do something absolutely amazing. They virtually slice off the ten horns and the little horn from the head of the fourth beast and *slide them down to the end of time!* Yet this creates an unnatural 1,500-year *gap* (more on this later) between the fourth beast, which is the Roman Empire, and the little horn. The truth is, the entire prophecy is orderly, successive, and chronological. There are four beasts, *then* ten horns, *then* the little horn—with *no gaps*. It is simply not logical, nor biblical, to slice a 1,500-year hole in the head of the fourth beast!

In Daniel's prophecies, "horns" also represent kingdoms (see Daniel 8:8, 22). What happened in history? In A.D. 476, the Roman Empire collapsed after being invaded by ten Germanic kingdoms from the north. These kingdoms laid the foundations of the modern nations of Europe—the Alemani (Germany), the Burgundians (Switzerland), the Saxons (England), the Visigoths (Spain), the Franks (France), the Lombards (Italy), and the Suevi (Portugal), as well as the Vandals, the Heruli, and the Ostrogoths. When the Roman imperial government collapsed in A.D. 476, Europe was looking for leadership. Can you guess who rose to supreme political power in the Roman Empire, "among" the ten horns, shortly "after" A.D. 476? *The Roman Catholic Church.*

Papal Rome was "different" from the powers that had gone before because it was not just a political power, but also a religious power. Three of the first ten horns (the Vandals, the Heruli, and the Ostrogoths) resisted papal Rome's rise to power. As a result of the Vatican's political influence, those three were destroyed and completely *"uprooted"* from history!

Papal Rome has "eyes like the eyes of a man," having human leadership centered in the pope. It has a "mouth speaking great things," when it claims to be the only true church, with the very keys of heaven and hell, outside of which there is no salvation. In September 2000, in his thirty-six-page document, *Dominus Jesus,* Pope John Paul II reaffirmed that there is salvation only in the Roman Church. Quickly the *Los Angeles Times* ran this headline: "Vatican Reiterates Strict Dogma—Roman Catholicism Only Path to Salvation, Declaration States." Thus, Rome's position has not changed, even in our modern times. It still has "a mouth speaking great things." This church *did indeed* make "war with the saints" by putting to death approximately 50 to 100 million so-called "heretics" during the Dark Ages. People today have forgotten about the Crusades, the dark torture chambers of the Inquisition, and the many horrifying massacres of Protestants and Jews. Yet these things really happened. Like a key fitting into a lock, so prophecy fits with history. It is also true that history unlocks prophecy.

Apart from Jesus Christ, more books have been written about Martin Luther than any other single religious person in history. How did Martin Luther interpret Daniel 7? Luther wrote that Daniel "saw the terrible wild beast which had ten horns, which by the consent of all is the Roman empire, he also beheld another small horn come up in the middle of them. *This is the Papal power,* which rose up in the middle of the Roman empire" (quoted in *Romanism and the Reformation: From the Standpoint of Prophecy,* H. Grattan

Guinness, Harley House, Bow, London. 1891, p. 127. Italics in original. See also *Works of Martin Luther,* vol. ii, p. 386). As bold and fiery as he was, Martin Luther did not slice a 1,500-year hole in the head of the fourth beast! He saw *no gap.*

Now back to the beast. A careful study of the Bible reveals that the beast of Revelation 13 is the same power as the little horn of Daniel 7. Most Catholics, Protestants, and Evangelicals, including the authors of *Left Behind,* agree with this. Again, it is their *interpretations* that vary. The Bible says the beast will be a composite creature with the characteristics of a lion, a bear, and a leopard (Revelation 13:2). It also has a mouth (verse 5), makes war on the saints (verse 7), and rules for forty-two months (verse 5), all of which are perfect parallels with Daniel 7. But there is something many people have missed that from a prophetic standpoint is a truth more important than avoiding quadruple bypass surgery. Here it is. Based on the perfect parallels of Revelation 13 with Daniel 7, *a beast represents a kingdom, not one man like Nicolae Carpathia!* And the Roman Catholic Church *is* a kingdom, with over one hundred embassies on Vatican Hill.

Revelation 13:2 mentions a lion, a bear, a leopard, and a dragon. While Satan is the primary dragon in the Bible, this verse clearly runs parallel with Daniel 7:3-7. The fourth beast in Daniel 7, which was dragon-like, was the Roman Empire. Revelation 13:2 says the dragon would give *"his seat"* to the beast. This "seat" does not refer to a physical chair somewhere, but rather to a seat of government. Where was the seat of government for the fourth beast? It was the city of Rome itself, and this is where the Vatican "sits" today! About 1,500 years ago, the Roman Empire gave its seat of government to the Roman Catholic Church. Notice this quotation from a well-known historian: "Disregarding the maxims and the spirit of the gospel, the papal church, arming herself with the power of the sword, vexed the church of God and wasted it for several centuries, a period most appropriately termed in history, the 'dark ages.' The kings of the earth, gave their power to the 'beast' " (*Fox's Book of Martyrs,* 1926 edition, p. 43).

As this book races down the highway of prophecy, it is essential that we pass through a major intersection—2 Thessalonians 2. The issues in that chapter are simply too great to pass by. There, Paul predicts the rising of "that man of sin" (verse 3). Doesn't this prove that the Antichrist is one man? That chapter is also used to support the idea of a secret Rapture *prior* to the coming of the Antichrist. Thus, this is a very important, controversial, and high-impact section of Scripture. As we examine it closely, we will discover some absolutely shocking truths. So put on your seat belts! Here we go!

It is almost unbelievable, but the very first line of 2 Thessalonians 2 actually disproves popular ideas. Paul wrote about "the coming of our Lord Jesus Christ" and "our gathering together to him" (verse 1). "Our gathering" clearly refers to the rapture of the church, but when does this gathering take place? At "the coming of our Lord Jesus Christ." What Greek word does Paul use here for "coming"? *Parousia!* This exact same word, *parousia,* is also used in verse 8, which speaks of the "brightness of his coming [*parousia*]." A simple comparison of verse 1 with verse 8 proves two things beyond question: (1) *Parousia* refers to the visibly "bright" and ultra-glorious Second Coming of Jesus Christ (as in Matthew 24:27, 30, 31) and (2) It is at this bright and highly visible Second Coming that Jesus will gather His church.

After referring to the "coming" or *parousia* of our Lord Jesus Christ, and our "gathering together to him," Paul solemnly warned: "Let no man deceive you by any means: for that day shall not come, except there come a *falling away first,* and that man of sin be revealed, the son of perdition" (verse 3, emphasis supplied). These words are power-packed! Here are the fast facts:

1. This passage is speaking about the Antichrist.
2. The Antichrist will arise as a result of "a falling away." The Greek word for "falling away," is *apostasia,* or "apostasy," and means *a falling away from grace and truth inside the church*!

3. This apostasy, resulting in the rise of the Antichrist, must come "first," that is, *before* "our gathering" to Jesus Christ. *Thus, the Antichrist definitely comes before the Rapture*!
4. It is Christians themselves who are in danger of being deceived about this, for Paul warned, "Let no man deceive *you* by any means" (verse 3, emphasis supplied).
5. Antichrist is "the son of perdition," which is a phrase Jesus applied to Judas in John 17:12. Judas was a professed Christian within the inner circle of Christ's followers. Thus, the Antichrist will not be someone like Nicolae Carpathia, but will be *a professed follower of Jesus Christ!* Judas even kissed Jesus, saying, "Hail, master" (Matthew 26:49), yet it was a kiss of betrayal.
6. The Antichrist is called "that man of sin," which is the same as the little horn which had "eyes like the eyes of a man" (Daniel 7:8). Daniel did not say the horn would *be* only one man, but that it would have "eyes *like* the eyes of a man." This is a subtle, and yet highly significant, difference.

Continuing his description of the Antichrist, Paul wrote: "Who opposeth and exalteth himself above all that is called God, or that is worshipped: so that he as God sitteth in the temple of God, shewing himself that he is God" (2 Thessalonians 2:4). Many apply this to a Nicolae Carpathia-type of Antichrist whom they think will someday enter a rebuilt Jewish temple in Israel, sit down, and boldly proclaim, "I am God." Yet is this what Paul is really saying? If you look at any concordance, you will discover that the Greek word used here for "temple" is *naos.* Paul used the very same word in 1 Corinthians 3:16. Writing to "the church of God" (1 Corinthians 1:2), Paul asked, "Know ye not that *ye are the temple of God?"* (italics supplied). The temple of God is the church, and this is where the Antichrist will sit! This doesn't mean that the Antichrist will literally sit down on some chair inside a physical building. To "sit" means to sit in a position of supreme authority. Jesus is now "seated" at the right hand of God. The Antichrist will "sit" in God's temple, which means he will sit in a position of supreme and apparently infallible authority *inside* the Christian church. Thus, the Antichrist will direct the eyes of people to himself in the place of Jesus Christ. The battle is between "that man of sin" and "the man Christ Jesus." The Antichrist will not blatantly *say,* "I am God," for this would be much too obvious and nonseductive. Rather, the Antichrist will sit *"as* God . . . *shewing himself* that he is God" (verse 4, emphasis supplied) by his statements and claims.

The Antichrist will sit in "the temple of God." Millions are now applying this to a rebuilt temple in Jerusalem, and this is one reason why American Christians are so interested in the latest news about the Israelis and the PLO. Yet think about it. If the Jews do rebuild their temple and start offering sacrifices, would this temple really be "the temple of *God*"? When Jesus Christ died, He "[caused] the sacrifice . . . to cease" (Daniel 9:27). He was the final sacrifice. If the Jews ever do resume animal sacrifices, what kind of statement would this be making to the Father? It would be an official denial of His Son! Therefore (are you ready for this?), that temple itself would be an *antichrist temple!* Honestly, could such a temple—which would be, in itself, a denial of Jesus—ever be properly called "the temple of *God*"? Never! (For more information on this subject, see my book, *Exploding the Israel Deception,* chapter 8, Titanic Truths about the Temple.)

Paul told the Thessalonians, "You know what is restraining, that he may be revealed in his own time" (2 Thessalonians 2:6, NKJV). Another extremely controversial issue is: "What (or who) is the restrainer holding back the Antichrist?" Many popular Bible teachers believe the "restrainer" is the Holy Spirit inside the Christian church. According to this theory, the Antichrist cannot come as long as the church remains in this world. Only after the church is "taken out of the way" (verse 7) in the Rapture can Antichrist appear. Yet think about it. If the Holy Spirit is removed from the earth at the Rapture, along with the church, then how could there ever be a Tribulation Force of new believers? There would be no Holy Spirit left on earth to convert anyone! And if somehow the Holy Spirit is still in this world after the Rapture, wouldn't He then be dwelling in the Tribulation Force? He would have to be, because the Bible says no man can resist Antichrist without the Holy Spirit dwelling *inside* him (1 John 4:4, 5). So, why wouldn't the Holy Spirit, dwelling inside the Tribulation Force after the Rapture, restrain the Antichrist? Why would the Holy Spirit restrain him inside a pre-Tribulation church, yet not be able to do so inside a post-Tribulation church? *There is something wrong with this picture!*

Paul continued his description of the Antichrist when he wrote: "The mystery of iniquity doth already work" (2 Thessalonians 2:7). According to these words, the Antichrist was "already" at work in Paul's day. Verse 8 says, "And then shall that Wicked be revealed, whom the Lord shall consume with the spirit of his mouth, and shall destroy with the brightness of his coming [*parousia*]." Thus, the Antichrist will continue to the visible return of Jesus Christ. This means that the Antichrist *started* in the time of Paul and will *continue* to the end, which makes it *impossible* for the Antichrist to be only one man! Not only that, it is at the bright and visible return of Jesus, at the *parousia* (see verse 8), when Christ will destroy the Antichrist and "gather" His church (verse 1), therefore, it is also *impossible* for the church to be the restrainer!

Who, then, is the restrainer? We must put Paul's words under a microscope to catch the right clues. Paul told the Thessalonians, "Do you not remember that when I was still with you *I told you* these things? And now *you know* what is restraining" (verses 5, 6, NKJV, emphasis supplied). Do you see it? The early church did know who the restrainer was, for Paul plainly says he had told them. Therefore, in order for us to know who the restrainer is, we must *go back* into ancient history and find out what the early church actually said about this subject, rather than looking to modern interpreters. When we do this, the answer becomes very clear.

H. Grattan Guiness, who has been called England's greatest teacher of prophecy wrote:

> The early church tells us what it did know about the subject, and no one in these days can be in a position to contradict its testimony as to what Paul had, by word of mouth only, told the Thessalonians. It is a point on which ancient tradition alone can have any authority. Modern speculation is positively impertinent on such a subject. . . . From *Irenaeus,* who lived close to apostolic times, down to *Chrysostom and Jerome,* the Fathers taught that the power withhold-

> ing the manifestation of the "man of sin" was *the Roman empire as governed by the Caesars*. . . . While the Caesars held imperial power, it was impossible for the predicted antichrist to arise, and that on the fall of the Caesars he *would* arise (*Romanism and the Reformation*, pp. 105-107, italics in the original). Therefore, the early church believed the restrainer was *the Roman Empire ruled by the Caesars*.

Why didn't Paul just come right out and tell us this in his letter? Wouldn't that have solved a lot of problems? Actually, there is a good reason why he didn't. The Thessalonians were already going though persecutions from the Roman Empire (see 2 Thessalonians 1:4). If this letter had specified that the Roman Empire would someday be "taken out of the way," this might have caused even more problems for those early believers. What if this letter fell into the wrong hands? If the Roman authorities discovered that these Christians believed the Roman Empire would eventually fall, they would have considered this high treason against Caesar! Again the cry would ring out, "To the Coliseum with the Christians!" So, in order to protect them, Paul told them privately without writing it down.

> Paul did not identify the restraining power which they knew to be Rome, for

> fear of reprisals. Remember the Christian church was under persecution by Rome. If the Thessalonian Christians were aware of Daniel seven, showing the rise of the "little horn" after the fourth kingdom of Rome (see Daniel 7:8, 24), then *the restraining power of Rome* against the revelation of the *Great Apostasy* of the Christian church made sense (*Champions of Christianity in Search of Truth,* by Ron Thompson, Teach Services, Inc. Brushton, New York. 1996. p. 47, italics in the original).

When the early church Fathers wrote about the restrainer, they used the secret code words of Scripture: *"The restrainer is the fourth beast of Daniel 7,"* which they knew was the Roman Empire. This is what Paul whispered when he "told" them, and this fits the prophecy perfectly. Daniel 7 predicted that after the fourth beast fell, *then* the little horn would appear, and historically that's what happened. When the Caesars went down, the popes came up to full power, and the Antichrist was revealed.

Martin Luther, John Calvin, and John Wesley, along with countless others, all believed "that man of sin," described in 2 Thessalonians 2:3, applied to the papal office of "the pope, sitting as God in the temple of God" (*History of the Reformation of the Sixteenth Century,* J. H. Merle d'Aubingne, book I, ch. III, p. 17). Martin Luther "proved, by the revelations of Daniel and St. John, *by the epistles of Paul,* and St. Jude, that the reign of Antichrist, predicted and described in the Bible, was the Papacy" (Ibid, book VI, ch. XII, p. 215, italics supplied). As with the prophecy of Daniel 7, all of the major Protestant Reformers interpreted Paul's prophecy in 2 Thessalonians 2 to be historical, chronological, and successive, with *no gaps.*

The Westminster Confession of Faith (1647), ratified and established by an act of the British Parliament, declares: "There is no other head of the church but the Lord Jesus Christ: nor can the Pope of Rome, in any sense be head thereof; but is that Antichrist, that man of sin and son of perdition, that exalteth himself in the church against Christ, and all that is called God" (*The Creeds of Christendom, With a History and Critical Notes,* Phillip Schaff, New York: Harper & Brothers, 1919, III, chap. 25. sec. 6. p. 658, 659). It is only fair to say that Rome is not alone in its problem of self-exaltation above Jesus Christ. This was Lucifer's original sin, and every true Christian struggles with this temptation as well. Catholics, Protestants, Evangelicals, Muslims, Jews, and Steve Wohlberg all need to gain the victory over pride *through the grace of God.* When it comes to basic human sin, we are all in this together.

Here's a simple summary of 2 Thessalonians 2: In Paul's own day, the "mystery of iniquity" was already at work (verse 7). The "falling away" had begun, and "that man of sin" was beginning to rise. But the Roman Empire with it's Caesars was restraining the Antichrist's rise to full power. In A.D. 476, when imperial Rome fell, being "taken out of the way," then the popes rose up as the main power brokers of Europe, and the Antichrist was revealed. The Antichrist will continue until the end of the world; then Jesus Christ will return with the "brightness of his coming," destroy the Antichrist, and gather His church to Himself. Who might belong to that church? In light of the context of 2 Thessalonians, it must be those who *have not fallen away from the truth!* Like the crackling of thunder, the voice of Paul cries out to us in the twenty-first century: "Let no man deceive you by any means"! The above interpretation is the only one that fully agrees with what Paul wrote and with what the early church actually said.

Off the coast of Florida, between Cuba and the Bermuda islands, exists a stretch of ocean called the Bermuda Triangle. Many ships have mysteriously vanished in those waters. No one knows why. When it comes to Bible prophecy, the ancient Protestant understanding of who the beast is has also largely vanished into the waves of history. Does anyone know why? Yes, many do, and in the next chapter you will join their ranks.

Then you will know *why* truth has been left behind.

CHAPTER

The Evil Empire of Jesuit Futurism

Imagine a pair of supernatural, high-tech, Heaven-inspired eyeglasses, which can give a Christian the instant ability to see one of Lucifer's greatest end-time deceptions. Such X-ray eyeglasses do exist. The purpose of this chapter is to help you find them and put them on so that you will be able to see and understand the almost unimaginable Evil Empire of *Jesuit Futurism.*

Modern Christianity has largely forgotten the importance of the Protestant Reformation, which took place during the 1500s:

> The sixteenth century presents the spectacle of a stormy sunrise after a dismal night. Europe awoke from long sleep of superstition. The dead arose. The wit-

> nesses to truth who had been silenced and slain stood up once more and renewed their testimony. The martyred confessors reappeared in the Reformers. There was a cleansing of the spiritual sanctuary. Civil and religious liberty were inaugurated. The discovery of printing and revival of learning accelerated the movement. There was progress everywhere. Columbus struck across the ocean and opened a new hemisphere to view. Rome was shaken on her seven hills and lost one-half of her dominions. Protestant nations were created. The modern world was called into existence (*Romanism and the Reformation,* p. 122).

For almost a thousand years Europe had been ruled by the iron hand of Rome. Only a few Bibles existed then, and Christianity was largely permeated with superstition. Faith in Jesus Christ, heart-felt appreciation for His love, and a simple trust in His death on the cross were almost unknown. The New Testament truth about grace, full forgiveness, and the free gift of eternal life to believers in the Son of God (see Romans 6:23) had been buried under a mass of tradition. Then, Martin Luther arose like a lion in Germany. After a period of tremendous personal struggle, Luther began teaching justification (being declared "just" by God) through faith in Jesus Christ, rather than through reliance on creature merits or any human works (Romans 1:16; 3:26, 28; 5:1).

Eventually, Martin Luther turned to the prophecies. By candlelight he read about the "little horn," the "man of sin," and "the beast." He was shocked as the Holy Spirit spoke to his heart. Finally, he saw the truth and said to himself, "Why, these prophecies apply to the Roman Catholic Church!" As he wrestled with this new insight, the voice of God echoed loudly in his soul, saying, "Preach the word" (2 Timothy 4:2)! And so, at the risk of losing his life, Martin Luther preached to an astonished people, publicly and in print, that papal Rome was indeed the Antichrist of Bible prophecy. Because of this dual message of salvation through faith in Jesus Christ apart from works *and* of papal Rome being the Antichrist, the river of history literally changed its course. Hundreds of thousands of people in Europe and in England left the Catholic Church.

" 'There are two great truths that stand out in the preaching that brought about the Protestant Reformation,' American Bible Commentator, Ralph Woodrow, reminds us; 'The just shall live by faith, not by the works of Romanism, and the Papacy is the Antichrist of Scripture.' It was a message for Christ and against Antichrist. The entire Reformation rests upon this twofold testimony" (*All Roads Lead to Rome,* Dorchester House Publications, Dorchester House, England, pp. 202, 203). It has been said that the Reformation first discovered Jesus Christ, and then in the blazing light of Christ, *it discovered the Antichrist*. This mighty Spirit-filled movement, *for* Christ and *against* the Antichrist, shook the world.

H. Grattan Guiness wrote these memorable words:

> From the first, and throughout, that movement [the Reformation] was energized and guided by the prophetic word. Luther never felt strong and free to war against the Papal apostasy till he recognized the pope as antichrist. It was then that he burned the Papal bull. Knox's first sermon, the sermon that launched him on his mission as a reformer, was on the prophecies concerning the papacy. The reformers embodied their interpretations of prophecy in their confessions of faith, and Calvin in his "Institutes." All of the reformers were unanimous in the matter, even the mild and cautious Melanchthon was as assured of the anti-papal meaning of these prophecies as was Luther himself. And their interpretation of these prophecies determined their reforming action. It led them to protest against Rome with extraordinary strength and undaunted courage. It nerved them to resist the claims of the apostate church to the utmost. It made them martyrs; it sus-

> tained them at the stake. And the views of the Reformers were shared by thousands, by hundreds of thousands. They were adopted by princes and peoples. Under their influence nations abjured their allegiance to the false priest of Rome. In the reaction that followed, all the powers of hell seemed to be let loose upon the adherents of the Reformation. War followed war: tortures, burnings, and massacres were multiplied. Yet the Reformation stood undefeated and unconquerable. God's word upheld it, and the energies of His almighty Spirit. It was the work of Christ as truly as the founding of the church eighteen centuries ago; and the revelation of the future which he gave from heaven—that prophetic book with which the Scripture closes—was one of the mightiest instruments employed in its accomplishment (*Romanism and the Reformation,* pp. 136, 137).

In 1545, the Catholic Church convened one of its most famous councils in history. It took place north of Rome in a city called Trent. The Council of Trent actually continued for three sessions, ending in 1563. One of the main purposes of this council was to plan a counterattack against Martin Luther and the Protestants. Thus, the Council of Trent became a center for

Rome's Counter-Reformation. Up to this point, Rome's main method of attack had been largely frontal—openly burning Bibles and heretics. Yet this warfare only confirmed in the minds of Protestants the conviction that papal Rome was indeed the beast power that would "make war with the saints" (Revelation 13:7) Therefore a new tactic was needed, something less obvious. This is where the Jesuits come in.

On August 15, 1534, Ignatius Loyola founded a secret Catholic order called the Society of Jesus, also known as the Jesuits. Historically, we might compare this order to Darth Vader's Evil Empire in the classic *Star Wars* films. The Jesuits definitely have a dark history of intrigue and sedition. That is why they were expelled from Portugal (1759), France (1764), Spain (1767), Naples (1767), and Russia (1820). "Jesuit priests have been known throughout history as the most wicked political arm of the Roman Catholic Church. Edmond Paris, in his scholarly work, *The Secret History of the Jesuits,* reveals and documents much of this information" (*Seventy Weeks: The Historical Alternative,* Robert Caringola, Abundant Life Ministries Reformed Press, 1991, p. 31). At the Council of Trent, the Catholic Church gave the Jesuits the specific assignment of destroying Protestantism and bringing people back to the Mother Church. This was to be done, not only through the Inquisition and through torture, but also through theology.

It's time to discover those X-ray eyeglasses. At the Council of Trent, the Jesuits were commissioned by the pope to develop a new interpretation of Scripture that would counteract the Protestant application of the Bible's prophecies regarding the Antichrist to the Roman Catholic Church. Fransico Ribera (1537-1591), a brilliant Jesuit priest and doctor of theology from Spain, basically said, "Here am I, send me." Like Martin Luther, Francisco Ribera also read by candlelight the prophecies about the Antichrist, the little horn, the man of sin, and the beast of Revelation. Yet he came to conclusions vastly different from those of the Protestants. "These prophecies don't apply to the Catholic Church at all," Ribera said. Then to whom do they apply? Ribera proclaimed: "To a single sinister man who will rise up at the end of time!" "Fantastic!" was Rome's reply, and this viewpoint was quickly adopted as the Church's official position on the Antichrist.

> In 1590 Ribera published a commentary on the Revelation as a counter interpretation to the prevailing view among Protestants which identified the Papacy with the Antichrist. Ribera applied all of Revelation but the earliest chapters to the end time rather than to the history of the church. Antichrist, he taught, would be a single evil person who would be received by the Jews and who would rebuild

> Jerusalem (George Eldon Ladd, *The Blessed Hope. A Biblical Study of the Second Advent and the Rapture*, Grand Rapids, Mich.: Eerdmans, 1956, 37-38).

> Ribera denied the Protestant Scriptural Antichrist (2 Thessalonians 2) as seated in the church of God—asserted by Augustine, Jerome, Luther, and many reformers. He set on an *infidel Antichrist, outside the church of God.* (*Champions of Christianity in Search of Truth*, p. 89, italics in the original).

The result of his [Ribera's] work was a twisting and maligning of prophetic truth (*Seventy Weeks: The Historical Alternative*, p. 32).

Following close behind Francisco Ribera was another brilliant Jesuit scholar, Cardinal Robert Bellarmine (1542-1621) of Rome. Between 1581-1593, Cardinal Bellarmine published his "Polemic Lectures Concerning the Disputed Points of the Christian Belief Against the Heretics of This Time." In these lectures he agreed with Ribera. "The futurist teachings of Ribera were further popularized by an Italian cardinal and the most renowned of all Jesuit controversialists. His writings claimed that Paul, Daniel, and John had nothing whatsoever to say about the Papal power. The futurists' school won general acceptance among Catholics. They were taught that antichrist was a single individual who would not rule until the very end of time" (*Great Prophecies of the Bible,* Ralph Woodrow, p. 198). Through the work of these two clever Jesuit scholars, we might say that a brand new baby was born into the world. Protestant historians have given this baby a name—Jesuit futurism. In fact, Francisco Ribera has been called the Father of Futurism.

Before we go much further, let's define some terms. *Historicism* is the belief that biblical prophecies about the little horn, the man of sin, the Antichrist, the beast, and the Babylonian harlot of Revelation 17, all apply to *the developing history of Christianity and to the ongoing struggle between Jesus Christ and Satan within the church,* culminating at the end of time. Historicism sees these prophecies as having a direct application to papal Rome *as a system* whose doctrines are actually a denial of the New Testament message of free salvation by grace through simple faith in Jesus Christ, apart from works. Historicism was the primary prophetic viewpoint of the Protestant Reformation. In direct opposition to historicism, and rising up as a razor-sharp counterattack against Protestantism, was the Jesuit viewpoint of futurism. Futurism basically says, "The Antichrist prophecies have nothing to do with the history of papal Rome, rather, they apply to *only one sinister man* who comes at the end of time."

Thus, Jesuit futurism sweeps fifteen hundred

years of prophetic history under the proverbial rug by inserting its infamous *gap.* The *gap* theory teaches that when Rome fell, prophecy stopped, only to continue again right around the time of the Rapture. Thus the ten horns, the little horn, the beast, and the Antichrist *have nothing to do with Christians today.* According to this viewpoint, how many prophecies were being fulfilled during the Dark Ages? None. Zero.

For almost 300 years after the Council of Trent, this Catholic baby (Jesuit futurism) remained largely inside the crib of Catholicism, but the plan of the Jesuits was that this baby would grow up and *finally be adopted by Protestants.* This adoption process actually began in the early 1800s in England, and from there it spread to America. The story of how this happened is both fascinating and tragic. As I briefly share some of the highlights, I want to clarify that many of the individuals I will mention were (and are) genuine Christians. Yet is it possible for a Christian to unknowingly become a channel for error? Can a sincere Christian be used by both Jesus Christ and the devil? At first we might say, "Never!" But consider this. Jesus told Peter that God was blessing him as he shared his faith in Christ (Matthew 16:15-17) and then, just a few minutes later, Peter yielded to temptation, and Satan spoke through him (verses 21-23)! This proves that a Christian can be used by both God and Lucifer, and all within a short space of time. I call this the "Peter Principle."

"The Futurism of Ribera never posed a positive threat to the Protestants for three centuries. It was virtually confined to the Roman Church. But early in the nineteenth century it sprang forth with vehemence as it latched on to Protestants of the Established Church of England" (*Champions of Christianity in Search of Truth,* p. 91). Dr. Samuel Roffey Maitland (1792-1866), a lawyer and Bible scholar, became a librarian to the Archbishop of Canterbury. It is very likely that he came upon Ribera's commentary in the library. In any event, in 1826 he published a widely read book attacking the Reformation and supporting Ribera's idea of a future one-man Antichrist. For the next ten years, in tract after tract, he continued his anti-Reformation rhetoric. As a result of his zeal and strong attacks against the Reformation in England the Protestantism of that very nation, which produced the King James Bible (1611), received a crushing blow.

After Maitland came James H. Todd, a professor of Hebrew at the University of Dublin. Todd accepted the futuristic ideas of Maitland, publishing his own supportive pamphlets and books. Then came John Henry Newman (1801-1890), a member of the Church of England and a leader of the famous Oxford Movement (1833-1845). In 1850, Newman wrote his "Letter on Anglican Difficulties" revealing that one of his goals in the Oxford Movement was to finally absorb "the various English denominations and parties" back into the Church of Rome. After publishing a pamphlet endorsing Todd's futurism about a one-man Antichrist, Newman soon became a full Roman Catholic and later even a highly-honored cardinal. Through the influence of Maitland, Todd, Newman, and others, a definite "Romeward movement was already arising, destined to sweep away the old Protestant landmarks, as with a flood" (H. Grattan Guinness, *History Unveiling Prophecy or Time as an Interpreter,* New York: Fleming H. Revell Co., 1905, p. 289).

Then came the much-respected Scottish Presbyterian minister Edward Irving (1792-1834), the acknowledged forerunner of both the Pentecostal and charismatic movements. Irving pastored the large Chalcedonian Chapel in London with over 1,000 members. When Irving turned to the prophecies, he eventually accepted the one-man Antichrist ideas of Todd, Maitland, Bellarmine, and Ribera, yet he went a step further. Somewhere around 1830 Edward Irving began to teach the unique idea of a two-phase return of Christ, *the first phase being a secret rapture prior to the rise of the Antichrist.* Where he got this idea is a matter of much dispute. Journalist Dave MacPherson believes Irving accepted it is a result of a prophetic revelation given to a young Scottish girl named Margaret McDonald (Dave MacPherson, *The Incredible Cover-Up: Exposing the Origins of Rapture Theories.* Omega Publications, Medford

Oregon. 1980). Wherever he got it, the fact is, he taught it!

In the midst of this growing anti-Protestant climate in England, there arose John Nelson Darby (1800-1882). A brilliant lawyer, pastor, and theologian, Darby wrote more than fifty-three books on Bible subjects. A much-respected Christian and a man of deep piety, he took a strong stand in favor of the infallibility of the Bible in contrast with the liberalism of his day. He became one of the leaders of a group in Plymouth, England which became known as the Plymouth Brethren. Darby's contribution to the development of evangelical theology has been so great that he has become known as the father of modern dispensationalism. Yet John Nelson Darby, like Edward Irving, also became a strong promoter of a pre-Tribulation rapture followed by a one-man Antichrist. In fact, this teaching has become a hallmark of dispensationalism.

Dispensationalism is the theory that God's dealings with mankind are divided into major sections or time periods. According to Darby, we are now in the "Church Age," that is, until the Rapture. After the Rapture, the seven-year period of Daniel 9:27 will supposedly kick in, when the Antichrist will rise up against the Jews. In fact, John Nelson Darby laid much of the foundation for the present popular idea of removing Daniel's seventieth week from its historical context in the time of Jesus Christ and applying it to a future tribulation after the Rapture.

Thus, in spite of all the positives of his ministry, Darby followed Maitland, Todd, Bellarmine, and Ribera by incorporating the teachings of futurism into his theology. This created a link between John Nelson Darby, the father of dispensationalism, and the Jesuit Francisco Ribera, the father of futurism. Darby visited America six times between 1859 and 1874, preaching in all of its major cities, during which time he planted the seeds of futurism in American soil. The child of the Jesuits was growing up.

One of the most important figures in this whole drama is Cyris Ingerson Scofield (1843-1921), a lawyer from Kansas, who was greatly influenced by the writings of Darby. In 1909, Scofield published the first edition of his famous Scofield Reference Bible. In the early 1900s, this Bible became so popular among American Protestants that it was necessary to print literally millions of copies. Yet, in the much-respected footnotes of this very Bible, Scofield injected large doses of the fluid of futurism also found in the writings of Darby, Todd, Maitland, Bellarmine, and Ribera. Through the Scofield Bible, the Jesuit child reached young adulthood. The doctrine of an Antichrist still to come was becoming firmly established inside twentieth-century American Protestantism.

The Moody Bible Institute and the Dallas Theological Seminary have strongly supported the teachings of John Nelson Darby, and this has continued to fuel futurism's growth. Then in the 1970s, pastor Hal Lindsey, a graduate of Dallas Theological Seminary, released his blockbuster book *The Late Great Planet Earth.* This 177-page, easy-to-read volume brought futurism to the masses of American Christianity and beyond. *The New York Times* labeled it, "The number one best-seller of the decade." Over 30 million copies have been sold, and it has been translated into more than thirty languages. Through *The Late Great Planet Earth,* the child of Jesuit futurism became a man.

Then came *Left Behind.* In the 1990s, Tim LaHaye and Jerry Jenkins took the future one-man Antichrist idea of Hal Lindsey, Scofield, Darby, Irving, Newman, Todd, Maitland, Bellarmine, and Ribera, and turned it into "The most successful Christian-fiction series ever," according to *Publishers Weekly.* Hal Lindsey's book, *The Late Great Planet Earth,* was largely theological, which limited its appeal, while *Left Behind* is a sequence of highly imaginative novels "overflowing with suspense, action and adventure," a "Christian thriller" with a "label its creators could never have predicted: blockbuster success," (*Entertainment Weekly*). The much-respected television ministries of Jack Van Impe, Peter and Paul Lalonde, and Pastor John Hagee have all worked together to produce *Left Behind: The Movie.* The entire project has even caught the attention of *The New York Times* and *The Wall Street Journal,* resulting in an interview of Tim LaHaye and Jerry Jenkins on *Larry King Live.* The *Left Behind* books have been made available at displays in Wal-Mart, Fry's Electronics, and other stores.

Again, let me clarify that I believe the authors of *Left Behind* and the leaders of these television ministries are genuine Christians who are doing their best to influence people for God's kingdom. God is using them, just like the Father spoke through Peter when he firmly confessed his faith in Christ (Matthew 16:15-17). Remember that "Peter Principle." There is much that is good in *Left Behind,* which God can use to influence people for Jesus Christ. Yet, in the full light of Scripture, prophecy, and the Protestant Reformation, something is terribly wrong. *Left Behind* is now teaching much of the very same Jesuit futurism of Francisco Ribera, which is hiding the real truth about the Antichrist. Through *Left Behind,* the floodgates of futurism have been opened, unleashing a massive tidal wave of false prophecy, which is now sweeping over America. Sadly, it is a false "idea whose time has come."

As we have already seen, the theological foundation for the entire *Left Behind* series is the application of the seven years of Daniel 9:27 to a future period of tribulation. Are you ready for this? Guess who was one of the very first scholars to slice Daniel's seventieth week away from the first sixty-nine weeks and slide it down to the end of time? It was the Jesuits' very own Francisco Ribera! "Ribera's primary apparatus was the seventy weeks. He taught that Daniel's seventieth week was still in the future. . . . It was as though God put a giant rubber band on this Messianic time measure. Does this supposition sound familiar? This is exactly the scenario used by Hal Lindsey and a multitude of other current prophecy teachers" (*Seventy Weeks: The Historical Alternative,* p. 35).

When most Christians look at the last 1,500 years, how much fulfilled prophecy do they see? None, zero. Because almost everything is now being applied to a future time period after the Rapture. As we have seen, this *gap* idea originated with the Jesuits, and its insertion into the majority of twenty-first century prophetic teaching is now blinding millions of hearts and eyes to what has gone before and to what is happening right now inside the church. "It is this GAP theory that permeates Futurism's interpretation of all apocalyptic prophecy" (*Champions of Christianity in Search of Truth,* p. 90). In love and in the Spirit of Jesus Christ, someone should publicly appeal to the major prophetic television ministries of today to re-evaluate their positions. Hopefully, like noble ships with a new command from their captains, they will yet change their courses.

Jesuit futurism has now become like a giant, seven-foot, 300-pound boxer, with spiked gloves. With an apparently all-powerful punch, it has almost knocked Protestant historicism entirely out of the ring. "The proper eschatological term for the view most taught today is *futurism* . . . which fuels the confusion of dispensationalism. The futuristic school of Bible prophecy came from the Roman Catholic Church, specifically her Jesuit theologians. . . . However the alternative has been believed for centuries. It is known as *historicism*" (Robert Caringola, *Seventy Weeks: the Historical Alternative*, p. 6). "It is a matter of deep regret that those who hold and advocate the futurist system at the present day, Protestants as they are for the most part, are thus really playing into the hands of Rome, and helping to screen the Papacy from detection as the Antichrist" (*Daniel and the Revelation: The Chart of Prophecy and Our Place In It, A Study of the Historical and Futurist Interpretation*, by Joseph Tanner, London: Hodder and Stoughton, 1898, p. 16).

Who had the right theology—those who were burned at the stake for Jesus Christ or those who lit the fires? Who had the true Bible doctrine—the martyrs or their persecutors? Who had the correct interpretation of the Antichrist—those who died trusting in the blood of Christ or those who shed the blood of God's dear saints? Dear friend, the Evil Empire of Jesuit Futurism is at war with the Protestant Reformation by denying its power-packed application of prophecy to the Vatican. "The futurist school of Bible prophecy was created for one reason, and one reason only:

to counter the Protestant Reformation!" (*Seventy Weeks: The Historical Alternative,* p. 34). In fact, this Evil Empire of Jesuit Futurism is at war with the prophecies of the Word of God itself! And if that's not enough, consider this: Jesuit futurism originated with the Roman Catholic Church itself, which makes it the very doctrine of the Antichrist! And when Christian ministries and movies like *A Thief in the Night, Apocalypse, Revelation, Tribulation,* and *Left Behind: The Movie* proclaim an Antichrist who comes only after the Rapture, what are they really doing? I shudder even to say it. Are you ready for this? They are sincerely and unknowingly teaching the doctrine of the Antichrist!

You have discovered those heavenly X-ray eyeglasses.

Now you understand *why* truth has been left behind.

CHAPTER

The Return of the Wounded Beast

The Bible says concerning the beast, "His deadly wound was healed: and all the world wondered after the beast" (Revelation 13:3). In the seventh of the *Left Behind* novels, after Antichrist Nicolae Carpathia is assassinated in Jerusalem, his corpse is jetted to New Babylon. The funeral service takes place before millions of viewers with full media coverage. As the world's television cameras are fixed on the coffin, the unbelievable occurs. Carpathia's left index finger begins to move; his chest starts to swell; his eyes open. Nicolae finally stands up and triumphantly declares before an awestruck world, "Peace be unto you!" (*The Indwelling—The Beast Takes Possession,* pp. 364-366). In the eighth book, "His Excellency Global Community Potentate Nicolae Carpathia is back, this time as Satan. Resurrected and indwelt by the devil himself, it's no more Mr. Nice Guy as the beast tightens his grip as ruler of the world" (*The Mark—The Beast Rules The World,* inside cover). This is how Christians today imagine that Revelation 13:3 might be fulfilled.

This literal view of a murdered and resurrected Antichrist has been depicted in scores of books on Bible prophecy and was graphically illustrated in the multimillion-dollar Christian film, *The Omega Code.* Although details vary, most modern portrayals involve the Antichrist being shot with a gun and then miraculously being raised to life. When Ronald Reagan survived a gunshot wound during his presidency, some speculated that he might be the Antichrist whose deadly wound was healed.

There is a big difference between fact and fiction. The wounding of the beast is referred to four times in Revelation (13:3, 10, 12, 14). The Bible mentions "the beast, which had the wound by a sword, and did live" (13:14). Thus, the beast is wounded by a sword, not a gun. Here is an additional insight: "He who leads into captivity shall go into captivity; he who kills with the sword must be killed with the sword" (verse 10). A simple comparison of verse 14 with verse 10 reveals the fascinating fact that the wounding of the beast also involves his going into captivity.

In order to understand this captivity correctly, we must analyze a special time period referred to briefly earlier in chapter 2 of this book. The little horn is predicted to rule for "a time and times and the dividing of time" (Daniel 7:25). A "time" represents one year, so this verse is talking about three and a half years. This same period is referred to as "forty-two months" (Revelation 13:5) or "one thousand two hundred and sixty days" (Revelation 12:6). Using thirty-day months, three and a half years equals forty-two months or 1,260 days. In symbolic prophecy, a day represents a literal year (see Ezekiel 4:6; Numbers 14:34). Almost all Catholic, Protestant, and Evangelical scholars, including the authors of *Left Behind,* apply this "day for a year" principle to the seventy-week or 490-day prophecy of Daniel 9:24-27. It is universally accepted that those 490 days represent 490 literal years. We know this is true because the prophecy of Daniel 9 begins in the time of Persia after the Babylonian captivity and reaches down to the time of Jesus Christ, the Messiah. Therefore, it must mean 490 literal years—not merely 490 actual days. We can nail this down for sure.

But when it comes to Daniel 7 with it's three-and-a-half-year period (Daniel 7:25), most modern interpreters shift their interpretative gears completely away from the day-year principle by applying this period to a literal three and a half years at the very close of time. Amazingly, this is exactly what the Jesuits Francisco Ribera and Cardinal Bellarmine did in their attempt to strategically remove the three and a half years from any connection with the Catholic Church. Yet Protestants of earlier days saw this quite differently. For almost 400 years, Protestant scholars applied the day-year principle, not only to the 490 days of Daniel 9, but also to the three and a half years of Daniel 7. They also applied it to the Vatican. "The seventy weeks of Daniel, or 490 days to Messiah, were fulfilled as 490 years; that is, they were fulfilled on the year-day scale. On this scale the forty-two months, or 1,260 days, are 1,260 years. We ask then, Has the Papacy endured this period? An examination of the facts of history will show that it has" (H. Grattan Guinness, *Romanism and the Reformation,* p. 84). In 1701, Robert Flemming published his book, *The Rise and Fall of Rome Papal.* "Fleming showed, as others had done for many centuries, that the 1,260 days of prophecy represent 1,260 years" (Ibid., p. 156.)

H. Grattan Guinness, in his monumental work, *Romanism and The Reformation,* marks the beginning of the 1,260 years with "the notable decree of the emperor Justinian [A.D. 525-565] constituting the Bishop of Rome as the head of all Churches" and then reaching down to the time of "the tremendous Papal overthrow in the French Revolution" (Ibid., p. 84). The decree of the eastern Roman emperor Justinian went into effect in A.D. 538. This made the bishop of Rome the legal "Head of all the Holy Churches," thus establishing the papacy's political power over all of Christianity in western Europe. Exactly 1,260 years later, in 1798, Napoleon's general, Berthier, entered Rome with a French army. Berthier promptly abolished the papacy, dismissed the Vatican's Swiss guards, and proclaimed Rome to be a republic for France.

"Berthier entered Rome on the 10th of February, 1798, and proclaimed a republic" (*The Modern Papacy,* p. 1, London: Catholic Truth Society). "One day the Pope was sitting on his throne in a chapel of the Vatican, surrounded by his cardinals. . . . Very soon a band of soldiers burst into the hall, who tore away from his finger his pontifical ring, and hurried him off, a prisoner" (*Epochs of the Papacy,* p. 449. London. 1881). Pope Pius VI was taken to France where he died in exile. "Napoleon gave orders that in the event of his death no successor should be elected to his office, and that the Papacy should be discontinued" (*The Modern Papacy,* p. 1). In 1798, "The Papacy was extinct: not a vestige of existence remained; and among all the Roman Catholic powers not a finger was stirred in its defense. The Eternal City had no longer prince or pontiff; its bishop was dying captive in foreign lands; and the decree was already announced that no successor would be allowed in his place" (*Rome: From the Fall of the Western Empire,* by George Trevor. pp. 439, 440. London: The Religious Tract Society. 1868). Notice that little word "captive" in the above sentence. It is the same word the Bible uses in Revelation 13:10.

The year 1798 was before the time of Dr. Samuel Maitland, Edward Irving, John Nelson Darby, C. I. Scofield, Hal Lindsey, and the producers of *Left Behind: The Movie.* Because at that time Protestant scholars all over Europe, England, and America were historicists, rather than futurists, they recognized the hand of God in the clear fulfillment of prophecy. In "the downfall of the papal government . . . many saw in these events the accomplishment of prophecies, and the exhibition of signs promised in the most mystical parts of the Holy Scriptures" (*History of France from 1790-1802*, vol. II, p. 379. London. 1803). "God's prophetic clock had set the year 1798 as the end of the papal supremacy, and when the hour struck, the mighty ruler on the Tiber, before whose anathemas the kings and emperors of Europe had so long trembled, went 'into captivity' (Revelation 13:10), and his government in the Papal States was abolished" (*Facts of Faith,* by Christian Edwardson. Southern Publishing Assoc., Nashville, Tenn., 1943, p. 60). At the end of the 1,260 years, in the year 1798, the biblical beast went into "captivity" and received its "deadly wound." This is fact, not fiction.

You've heard the expression, "You've come a long way, baby." This is especially true when it comes to prophetic interpretation. Best-selling books and blockbuster Christian movies now apply Revelation's prophecy of a beast that receives a deadly wound to some fictitious individual like Nicolae Carpathia who is assassinated after the Rapture. Yet this is all like a house of illusion at an amusement park. The Bible says the beast, which represents a kingdom (Daniel 7:23), would go into "captivity" (Revelation 13:10). The kingdom of papal Rome did go into captivity. And this happened in 1798, exactly at the end of the 1,260 years!

Yet as Paul Harvey so often says, we need to hear "the rest of the story." The Vatican did not come to a permanent end in 1798; neither does Revelation stop with the beast being wounded. God's Word predicts, "His deadly wound was healed: and all the world wondered after the beast" (Revelation 13:3). Is this happening now? There is no question about it! The former deadly wound inflicted upon papal Rome now hardly needs a bandaid. With over a billion members, the Roman Catholic Church is now the most powerful religious organization on planet Earth. When the pope addresses the United Nations, the global community listens. So why aren't more Protestants listening and seeing the fulfillment of prophecy? *Because they are waiting for Nicolae.*

In 1990, best-selling author Malachi Martin published his book, *The Keys of this Blood: Pope John Paul II Versus Russia and the West for Control of the New World Order.* Martin is a Jesuit, a Vatican insider, who knows the pope. Martin's theme is that only three powers are capable of ruling the world in the New World Order—Russia,

America, and the Vatican. Martin predicts Rome will win. Near the beginning of his book he significantly refers to "two hundred years of inactivity," which has "been imposed on the papacy by the major secular powers of the world." (*The Keys of this Blood,* p. 22). Do you realize the significance of this? Count back two hundred years from 1990. What year does this bring us to? To 1790, which is only eight years away from the inflicting of the wound! Martin continues by saying that after "some two hundred years of official nonexistence . . . the distinguishing mark of John Paul's career as Pontiff" has been to "throw off the straight jacket of papal activity in major world affairs" (Ibid., p. 23). Martin lifts the veil aside and reveals that Pope John Paul's ultimate goal is for the Vatican to once again rule the world.

There is no president, no statesman, or no rock-and-roll singer, including Mick Jaggar, Michael Jackson, or Madonna, who can gather a larger crowd than Pope John Paul II. In 1995, *Time* magazine named him its Man of the Year. "When he talks, it is not only to his flock of nearly a billion; he expects the world to listen. And the flock and the world listen" (*Time,* Dec. 26, 1994 / Jan. 1995). I am not writing any of this to question the pope's morals, integrity, or sincerity, nor am I qualified to determine his destiny. Personally, I like John Paul and would love to see him in heaven. But when it comes to prophecy, the fact remains that he represents a system that for 400 years Bible-believing Protestants have believed is represented by the beast power of Revelation. If Protestants were correct in this belief back then, then it is still a correct view today. Why? Because God's Word has not changed!

No doubt you have heard of the Seven Wonders of the Ancient World. These were magnificent structures, colossal monuments. One thinks of the Hanging Gardens of Babylon and of the Great Pyramid of Giza. In modern times, people stand amazed at the lightninglike developments of technology—computers, the Internet, satellite communications, fiber optics, and cell phones. Yet there is another "wonder" predicted in Revelation, which also applies to our modern times.

It concerns a wounded beast that is now healing.

And the world is wondering today.

CHAPTER 5

The United States in Bible Prophecy

The United States of America is now "the world's sole remaining superpower" (*Time,* July 29, 1991. p. 13). Washington, D.C. has appropriately been called, "the new Rome" (*Newsweek,* August 12, 1991. p. 33). The Bible clearly refers to the ancient nations of Babylon, Persia, Greece, and Rome. They were superpowers in their day and are mentioned in prophecy because they had a direct historical connection with God's chosen people. In our modern times, America, more than any other nation, has aided the spread of Christianity. In our national pledge, we still claim to be "One nation under God." Our coins still say, "In God We Trust." Therefore, it is appropriate to ask: Has America been left behind in Bible prophecy?

Revelation 13 actually describes two beasts. We have already discovered the irrefutable and immovable fact that in Bible prophecy, a beast represents a kingdom. "The fourth beast shall be the fourth kingdom upon earth" (Daniel 7:23). This point is of mega-importance when it comes to prophetic interpretation. It is also an irrefutable fact of history that for almost four hundred years Protestants have interpreted the first beast in Revelation 13 to represent the kingdom of papal Rome. But there is a second beast also mentioned in the same chapter. John wrote, "And I beheld another beast coming up out of the earth; and he had two horns like a lamb, and he spake as a dragon" (verse 11). Who is this second beast? Let's find out.

John saw "another beast" rising into power. Again, what does a beast represent? "The fourth beast shall be the fourth kingdom upon earth" (Daniel 7:23). Everyone admits that Daniel 7 parallels Revelation 13. Therefore, this second beast must also represent a great kingdom or nation. It also must be an end-time kingdom because the second beast is finally involved in the enforcement of that mysterious mark (Revelation 13:11-17). The second beast rises "out of the earth" whereas the first beast came out of the sea (Revelation 13:1). This often-overlooked detail is actually quite significant. In fact, all four beasts in Daniel 7 came out of the sea. What does "the sea" or water represent in prophecy? The Pacific

Ocean? Hardly. In Revelation 17:1, John saw a woman named "Babylon" sitting upon "many waters." An angel explained, "The waters which thou sawest, where the whore sitteth, are peoples, and multitudes, and nations, and tongues" (Revelation 17:15). Thus, the "water" represents lots of people. Historically, the great nations of Babylon, Persia, Greece, and Rome rose up from among the multitude of nations in Europe and the Middle East.

The second beast was seen "coming up out of the earth." If the "water" represents lots and lots of people, then "the earth" would represent a sparsely populated area—more of a wilderness region. The second beast is also described as being "like a lamb." In the Bible, a lamb is primarily a symbol of Jesus Christ (John 1:29; Revelation 14:1). The second beast is not Jesus, to be sure, but it will be lamb-like; it will be "like" Jesus in some significant way. It also has "two horns." Horns in prophecy represent either kings, kingdoms, or divisions within a kingdom (see Daniel 7:17, 23, 24; 8:3, 8, 20-22). Thus, the second beast might have a division of power within itself.

Also there is much more to the matter of the time when this beast arises than a simple appearance near the end time. The prophecy is more specific. On December 31, 1999, almost the whole world was thinking about time. Would the infamous Y2K computer bug lead to a global technological meltdown? On New Year's Eve, I was watching Peter Jennings and his ABC coverage. The countdown began—five, four, three, two, one . . . fizzle! Nothing happened. The year 2000 arrived with hardly a hiccup, yet when it comes to the time of the rise of the second beast, there is something much larger than a fizzle that should attract our attention. Speculative Y2K doomsday prophecies proved false, but true prophecy never fails.

In the last chapter we talked about the wounding of the first beast. This wound occurred on time in the exact year that marked the end of the 1,260 years. What year was that? 1798. This wound is described in Revelation 13:10. In that verse the first beast is described as going into "captivity." In other words, in 1798, he would be on his way down. Now notice, it is in the very next verse that the second beast is seen "coming up." It's like a prophetic teeter-totter. The first beast goes down, and then the second beast comes up. This "down and up" activity occurs right around the same time, therefore, we need to look for a great kingdom coming into power around the year 1798.

John Wesley founded the Methodist Church in England in the 1700s. Like most other Protestants in his day, he had absolutely no interest in the speculative fancies of Jesuit futurism. In the 1750s, as he was studying prophecy, he realized the 1,260-year period would soon come to an end. In 1754, he published his much-respected *New*

Testament with Explanatory Notes. After applying the first beast of Revelation 13:1-10 to the papacy, he contemplated the rise of the second beast. Underneath verse 11, John Wesley wrote, "Another . . . beast . . . But he is not yet come, though he cannot be far off; for he is to appear at the end of the forty-two months of the first beast. And he had two horns like a lamb—a mild, innocent appearance" (John Wesley, *Notes on Revelation,* 1754. p. 457). The founder of the Methodist Church was right on target! His footnotes here were more reliable than many of those of C. I. Scofield.

A lamb is a young animal, a baby sheep. The fact that this nation is described as being lamb-like around 1798 indicates that this would be a young nation at this time. All of the other recognizable beasts in Daniel 7 (the lion, the bear, and the leopard) were like hungry wild animals. The nations of Babylon, Persia, Greece, and Rome rose by conquering the previous nation in power. Yet the lamb-like beast was to rise differently, more peacefully. The fact that it has no crowns on its horns is also highly significant. The first beast of Revelation 13 has horns with crowns. Crowns represent kingly power, as in the European nations. Papal Rome did in fact rule over kings. Yet the lamb-like nation would try something new. It would have no crowns, thus it would be a nation without a king.

Revelation 13 predicts that the second beast will eventually become a superpower. How do we know this? Because this beast eventually has the capability to enforce the mark of the first beast upon "all" the peoples of the world (Revelation 13:16). Therefore, the second beast must grow from its comparatively small and peaceful beginnings into a mighty nation of superpower status with global influence. And yet, in spite of its lamb-like profession, it will eventually "[speak] as a dragon" (Revelation 13:11). This indicates a final denial of its principles, internal degradation, and the use of satanic force.

When I was a boy, I put together a lot of jigsaw puzzles. Revelation 13 is part of God's jigsaw puzzle. So let's put the pieces together:

1. What youthful nation was "coming up" into power in a wilderness area around 1798?
2. What new nation around 1798 was "like a lamb," Christian in its features, mild and peaceful, without needing to conquer another great nation in its ascent?
3. What nation now has "two horns," that is, a division of power within its government?
4. What nation in its form of government has no crowns, is without kingly power, being ruled constitutionally "by the people"?
5. And what great nation is now the world's only superpower in the twenty-first cen-

tury, capable of enforcing the Mark of the Beast upon "all" the world?

When it comes to golf, there is only one Tiger Woods. When it comes to Bible prophecy, there is only one nation that qualifies as the second beast of Revelation 13. You know which nation that is—the United States of America. Our Declaration of Independence from England was signed in 1776. Our Bill of Rights was ratified in 1791. We "came up" right on time, around 1798, when the first beast was going down. Through the courage of godly leaders and the providence of Almighty God, we have become a great nation. The United States of America is now the only superpower left on planet Earth.

What does the future hold? We have already seen that God's unerring Word predicts the healing of the wound of the first beast (the Roman Church). In our next chapter, we will discover that the Bible also describes the first beast (the Vatican) and the second beast (Protestant America) working together during the closing seconds of time.

CHAPTER

Talking Statues and the Image of the Beast

The "image of the beast" is referred to nine times in the book of Revelation (13:14, 15; 14:9, 11; 15:2; 16:2; 20:4). The Bible solemnly warns, "If any man worship the beast and his image, . . . The same shall drink of the wine of the wrath of God" (Revelation 14:9, 10). As we can see, this is a life or death subject. Therefore, it is highly appropriate to ask: What is this mysterious "image of the beast" really all about?

In the *Left Behind* novels, after Nicolae Carpathia is assassinated in Jerusalem, a gigantic statue is erected inside of New Babylon in honor of the global community's recently fallen hero. During the funeral, in front of millions of people, "The image began to move. . . . All eyes turned toward it in terror and word quickly spread throughout the courtyard that something was happening. . . . The image soon glowed red hot, and the smoke poured out so fast that it again formed clouds that darkened the sky. The temperature dropped immediately. . . . The image roared, 'Fear not and flee not! Flee not or you shall surely die!' " (*The Indwelling*, pp. 357, 358). Shortly after Nicolae Carpathia's devil-induced resurrection, official orders are given to "reproduce the image of His Excellency, the great statue . . . in all the major cities throughout the world" (*The Mark—The Beast Rules the World*, p. 82). Honestly, can you imagine something like this actually being reported on CNN?

Yet, this kind of literalism, which applies Revelation's prophecy concerning the image of the beast to a smoking, glowing, talking idol, is very common today. People envision a "great statue" to which most of the world bows down after the Rapture. In the *Left Behind* novels, the only Christians who have to deal with this horrific, talking monstrosity are the "Tribulation Force." All other Christians have been removed from earth at the Rapture. Thus, this wildly popular saga with its spectacular entertainment makes all nine references to the image of the beast in the book of Revelation completely irrelevant to the church today. Is it really true? Will a gigantic statue someday speak? And is it right to interpret this subject in such a way that it has nothing to do with Christians today? Let's find out.

In previous pages of this book, we have talked about the Reformation in the 1500s, the Catholic counter-reformation at the Council of Trent, and the assignment given to the Jesuits to counteract the teaching of Martin Luther and the Protestants who were at that time calling papal Rome the Antichrist. We have also discovered how, out of faithfulness to the pope, the brilliant Jesuits Francisco Ribera and Cardinal Bellarmine cleverly reapplied these prophecies, deflecting them from the Vatican by assigning them to a single evil man who would come at the end of time. But what about the prophecy of an image of the beast? Did either of these two Jesuits talk about it? Yes, Cardinal Bellarmine did, and he applied it to a talking statue. "Bellarmine, like Ribera, advocated the futurist interpretation of prophecy. He taught that antichrist would be one particular man . . . would pretend to be God, [and] would make a literal image speak" (*Romanism and the Reformation*, p. 147, italics supplied).

Without realizing it, the authors of *Left Behind* have adopted the literalism of Jesuit futurism in their interpretation of prophecy, yet Revelation clearly uses many symbols, which are not meant to be taken literally. As we have already seen, a beast in prophecy represents a kingdom (Daniel 7:23). Water represents people (Revelation 17:15). The lamb is a symbol for Jesus Christ (Revelation 13:8). The 490 days represent 490 years (Daniel 9:24). The great Babylonian mother of harlots (Revelation 17:5) represents a false church. Yet, in a attempt to remove all applications of Antichrist prophecies from the Vatican, Jesuit futurism often takes the symbol and makes it literal, thus destroying its true meaning and relevance to Christians today. Perhaps the greatest example of such unrealistic literalism is the application of the image of the beast to a glowing, smoking, talking statue.

> Futurism is literalism, and literalism in the interpretation of symbols is a denial of their symbolic character. It is an abuse and degradation of the prophetic word, and a destruction of its influence. It substitutes the imaginary for the real, the grotesque and monstrous for the sober and reasonable. It quenches the precious light which has guided the saints for ages; and kindles a wild, delusive marsh-fire in its place. It obscures the wisdom of divine prophecy [and] denies the true character of the days in which we live (*Romanism and the Reformation,* p. 163).

In the midst of honest intentions, the *Left Behind* project has actually replaced "the imaginary for the real, the grotesque and monstrous for the sober and reasonable." As we shall soon see, all literal-talking-statue interpretations of this prophecy are no more real than the talking tin man in *The Wizard of Oz.*

The most powerful religious organization in the world today is the Roman Catholic Church. The most powerful nation on earth is the United States of America. When we reject the fantasies of Jesuit futurism in favor of the sober realities of history and of Protestant historicism, we discover that these two superpowers are the primary actors in the intense drama of Revelation 13. The first beast represents papal Rome, and the second beast represents Protestant America. Revelation 13 is largely a story of Rome and the Star Spangled Banner, of the Vatican and Washington D.C. In the very center of Revelation 13, Jesus Christ inserts this cryptic phrase, "If any man have an ear, let him hear" (Revelation 13:9). Therefore, Jesus wants Christians today to "hear" and to understand this prophecy, rather than applying it to everyone else after we're gone.

A careful study of Revelation 13 reveals that the second beast (Protestant America) will eventually set up an "image" of the first beast (papal Rome). What does this mean? What is an image anyway? In the beginning, God said, "Let us make man in our image, after our likeness" (Genesis 1:26). Thus, an image is a likeness. When we look in a mirror, we may not like what we see, nevertheless, we will see an image or a likeness of ourselves. In 1776, Protestant America was very different in its beliefs and form of government from the Roman Catholic Church. Papal Rome is a monarchy ruled by the pope. America is a democracy ruled by the people. Although Protestants have largely forgotten this, much of the American doctrine of liberty of conscience developed as a reaction to the Catholic idea of required submission to Rome. Yet prophecy predicts a change. An image will be formed in America. A likeness to papal Rome will take place. Are you starting to get the picture?

Revelation 13 predicts that before the image is fully formed both beasts will start working together. In the 1500s the Protestant Reformation resulted in a bloody and painful divorce from the Roman Church. In 1776 this separation continued with the formation of the United States of America—a new, freedom-loving, and heavily Protestant nation. American democracy has long been viewed as being in definite contrast with the government of papal Rome. During our Civil War in the 1860s, Abraham Lincoln spoke much about the dangerous influences against freedom, which at that time were emanating from the Jesuits and from the Vatican. Yet in the 1960s things began to change. The American Catholic Council, Vatican II, improved relations considerably. Then with the election of John F. Kennedy, our first Catholic president, much of America's concerns about Catholicism began to disappear—just like the Christians disappear in *Left Behind*!

Yet according to Revelation 13, the beast is

still the beast. As the lessons of history continue to fade from memory, being left behind, prophecy predicts that Protestant America will eventually lead people back to Rome. The Bible says the second beast will "[cause] the earth and them which dwell therein to worship the first beast, whose deadly wound was healed" (Revelation 13:12). This verse has not yet been fully fulfilled. Yet the stage of cooperation is definitely in full swing.

The front cover of a 1992 issue of *Time* magazine showed a picture of Ronald Reagan and the pope. The headline read, "Holy Alliance: How Reagan and the Pope conspired to assist Poland's Solidarity movement and hasten the demise of Communism." The gist of the article was that Washington D.C. and the Vatican had cooperated in a successful endeavor leading to the collapse of communism in eastern Europe. "This was one of the greatest secret alliances of all time," said Richard Allen, Reagan's first national security advisor, who was part of the team that worked with the pope (*Time,* Feb. 24., 1992, p. 28). President Reagan also appointed America's first Ambassador to the Vatican. A few Protestants protested, yet their pleas were unheeded.

In the latter part of the twentieth century, a unique historical development took place. American Protestants and Catholics reached across a gulf formerly as large as the Grand Canyon, shook hands, and joined forces like never before.

Why? The main reason is obvious, yet there is another that lies hidden. Protestants and Catholics have come together out of a common concern about abortion, immorality, the breakdown of the American family, and the growing power of liberal influences in the media. In 1994, in an effort to help each other in the common struggle against evil, Evangelical and Catholic leaders signed the famous ECT document—*Evangelicals and Catholics Together: The Christian Mission in the Third Millennium*. Like a fast flying jet, this trend continues to gain speed. The Protestant Reformation is increasingly being replaced by the ecumenical movement. Separation is out, and cooperation is in. But in September 2000, in an official thirty-six-page document (*Dominus Jesus*) the papacy declared that salvation is still found only inside the Roman Catholic Church. *The Vatican has not changed.*

Let me clarify something. I am not against all cooperation in the battle against evil. Neither do I believe that all Protestant and Catholic leaders who advocate unity will be lost. Jesus Christ loves us all and God alone is the ultimate Judge. Yet I am also a student of prophecy, and there is something very important I want you to understand. It is more important than what happens to the stock market or who wins the Super Bowl. The main reason this growing cooperation between Catholics and Protestants is now going forward unchecked is that Protestants have accepted a new view of prophecy that has taken the eyes of Christians away from the Roman Catholic Church. That view is Jesuit futurism, which says that papal Rome is not the beast.

Now back to the image. An image is a reflection or a likeness of an original. The Bible reveals that Protestant America will "make an image to the beast, which had the wound by a sword, and did live" (Revelation 13:14). In other words, Protestant America is to become like the Roman Catholic Church in some significant way. In order to really understand this prophecy, we must take a closer look at the governments and basic principles of both beasts.

The Roman Catholic Church is a union of government and religion. The pope is not just the leader of a church, he is also the king of a monarchy. Vatican City is not part of Italy. It is an independent country with its own Swiss guard, its own coins, its own postal system. This hybrid church/state organization is officially recognized by governments around the world. There are over a hundred embassies on Vatican Hill. The Roman Catholic Church is not a democracy. Its popes are not elected by the people, but by the cardinals, who are appointed by the pope. All good Catholics are required to submit to the authority of the Church in order to remain in right standing with God. During the Dark Ages, when people rebelled against the Vatican, the popes used various methods to pressure the other state governments of Europe to enforce compliance with Rome. Thus papal Rome, in its very essence, is a union of church and state.

The government of the United States is quite different. The U.S. Constitution makes a separation between government and religion. The First Amendment to the Bill of Rights (1791) declares, "Congress shall make no law respecting an establishment of religion or prohibiting the free exercise thereof." This means that the Federal government is to stick to civil issues without meddling in the things of the Lord. The government is not to restrict religion, nor is it to enforce or "establish" religion. When it comes to a person's relationship with God, the use of force is out. This allows for a free church in a free state and protects religious freedom. Thus, the First Amendment of the U. S. Constitution definitely places the government of Protestant America in contrast to that of the Roman Catholic Church, which has always required submission to the pope.

In the first century, Christianity was separate from the government. The power of the early church did not reside in Caesar, but in those blazing beams of light that emanated from a lonely cross. Jesus Christ came into this midnight world of ours, switched on the light, and revealed to everyone the inexpressible love of the Father. It's true that Jesus did tearfully point out the dangers and consequences of sin, yet He never used force. He never compelled anyone to believe in Him. Every person was free to accept or reject Him. With outstretched arms, Jesus invited all to come to Him for salvation, free forgiveness, and rest of soul. Instead of force, He manifested His own love to reach the heart.

At the end of His holy life, Jesus freely allowed sinners to arrest, beat, whip, and punch Him in the face. Without fighting back, He allowed Himself to be tried, mocked, and condemned to death. When misguided religious leaders turned Him over to the state—to Pontius Pilate—no angry words fell from His lips. He finally allowed Roman soldiers to nail Him to a splintering piece of wood. As He was lifted up, almost naked, between heaven and earth, Jesus quietly breathed a prayer for His enemies, "Father, forgive them; for they know not what they do" (Luke 23:34). Six hours later He was dead. Yet it was not the nails that killed the Son of God. Jesus died of a ruptured heart, carrying the sins of the world. As the Lamb of God, Jesus Christ totally absorbed the sins of Catholics, Protestants, Jews, Muslims, and atheists. He absorbed your sins and mine.

A damp, dark tomb was not the end. A shining angel came down from heaven and rolled away the stone from over Christ's grave. Then the Son of God came forth fulfilling the words, " 'I am the resurrection and the life' " (John 11:25). A little later, the angel told some women, " 'He is not here, but is risen!' " (Luke 24:6). Then came the Day of Pentecost, and as the power of the Holy Spirit fell like fire from heaven upon the disciples of Jesus Christ, the good news began to spread with lightning speed (Acts 2). As the disciples lifted up the infinite love of Jesus for a lost world, thousands were converted in a day. Soon there were tens of thousands, then hundreds of thousands. I want to make this point very clear—the power of the early church did not lie in the government, but in the Cross (1 Corinthians 1:23, 24). Those early Christians did not seek help from Caesar in spreading the good news; the use of force was out. Through the Holy Spirit, and with the heart-warming power of Christ's love, which alone can reach the heart, they had all they needed, and their message turned the world upside down.

Now let's go back to prophecy. The second beast has "two horns like a lamb" (Revelation 13:11). The lamb in Revelation represents Jesus Christ. The second beast is not Jesus, yet it has a certain lamb-like or Christ-like characteristic. This special characteristic is described as "two horns." Now think about it. Real lambs do not have horns! Therefore these "two horns" must be symbolic of a special teaching of Jesus Christ. This teaching must have two dimensions and must have a certain two-fold reflection in the government of the second beast. Let me explain.

One day a group of crafty Pharisees asked

Jesus a question in an effort to "entangle him in his talk" (Matthew 22:15). "Is it lawful to give tribute unto Caesar, or not?" (verse 17). They reasoned that if our Lord said, "No, don't pay taxes to Caesar," they could accuse Him of sedition to the Roman authorities. If He said, "Yes, pay taxes to Caesar," they would accuse Him before the Jews for being supportive of Rome. They thought their trap was inescapable. They hardly realized they were talking to Someone with an infinite I.Q. "Jesus perceived their wickedness, and said, Why tempt ye me, ye hypocrites? Shew me the tribute money. And they brought unto him a penny. And he saith unto them, Whose is this image and superscription? They say unto him, Caesar's. Then saith he unto them, Render therefore unto Caesar the things which are Caesar's; and unto God the things that are God's" (verses 18-21). They were stumped!

In saying that people should give to Caesar the things that are Caesar's, and to God the things that are God's, Jesus Christ very clearly separated the things of Caesar from the things of God. Caesar represents the government. The things of God concern religion. In the government of ancient Rome, Caesar and religion were united. "Entangled" might be a better word. Christians were required to worship Caesar or be thrown to half-starved lions. When the Roman Empire was replaced by the Roman Church, this "entangled" situation continued. During the Dark Ages, those who refused to obey the pope were punished by the state. The words of Jesus to those tricky Pharisees condemn all of this. He separated the things of Caesar from the things of God, thus denying the right of government to enforce religion. This arrangement preserves freedom of religion against state control. This is a principle of the lamb. To reject this principle is to favor the governmental system of the Roman Catholic Church.

The Church of Rome is fundamentally opposed to the separation of government and religion. In 1864 the Vatican issued its famous *Syllabus of Errors*. Number 6 labeled as a heresy worthy of hell-fire the American idea that, "That the Church ought to be separate from the State, and the State from the Church" (Phillip Schaff, *The Creeds of Christendom*, vol. II, The Greek and Latin Creeds. New York: Harper and Brothers, 1877, p. 227). A few years later, in an official letter dated June 20, 1888, Pope Leo XIII referred to "that fatal principle of the separation of Church and state" (*The Great Encyclical Letters of Pope Leo XIII*, 1903, p. 159).

This principle of Jesus Christ separating government and religion became a mighty issue at the very beginning of the Reformation. For hundreds of years, papal Rome had been enforcing her religion. As the teachings of Martin Luther began to take root in Germany, the spirit of freedom moved strongly upon princes and people. In cooperation with the pope, the German emperor Charles V was determined to bring the new-born Reformation to a screeching halt. In 1529, a famous council was assembled in Spires, Germany, and a group of noble German princes who had accepted the teachings of Luther were in attendance. At Spires, these princes were told they could maintain their new religious convictions in their local territories, yet they could not seek any more converts from among the Catholics. In its practical effect, this would have stopped the progress of the Reformation entirely. The German princes were faced with a tremendous decision. Should they accept this proposal in order to keep the peace with the pope and the emperor, or should they, at the risk of being literally burned to ashes, resist the highest authorities of Europe?

As the Reformed princes met privately to consider their options, it was unexpectedly announced before the council that this proposal was about to be drawn up in the form of a royal decree. The princes were told they had absolutely no choice but to submit to the emperor and the pope. What should they do? A mighty moment in history had arrived. If CNN had been around back then, this council would have had full media coverage. It was then that these brave men of royalty appealed "from the report of the Diet [the council] to the word of God, and from the Emperor Charles to Jesus Christ, the King of kings and Lord of lords" (Merle J. D'Aubingne, *History of the Reformation of the Sixteenth Century,* Book XIII, Ch. VI, p. 520). These German princes drew up a magnificent protest, which they then presented with breathtaking courage before the assembled dignitaries of Germany. "We protest by these present, before God, our only Creator, Preserver, Redeemer, and Savior, and who will one day be our Judge, as well as before all men and all creatures, that we, for us and for our people, neither consent nor adhere in any manner whatsoever to the proposed decree, in anything that is contrary to God, to His holy word, to our right conscience, to the salvation of our souls. . . .

"What! We ratify this edict! We assert that when the Almighty God calls a man to His knowledge, this man nevertheless cannot receive the knowledge of God! . . . We are resolved, with the grace of God, to maintain the pure and exclusive preaching of His only word, such as is contained in the biblical books of the Old and New Testaments. . . . This word is the only truth; it is the sure rule of all doctrine and of all life, and can never fail or deceive us. He who builds on this foundation shall stand against all the powers of hell, while all the human vanities that are set up against it shall fall before the face of God. . . . For this reason we reject the yoke that is imposed upon us" (Ibid.) Silence fell upon that vast assembly! The Holy Spirit spoke with power to those heads of church and state. One of the greatest protests in history had just been heard. Most modern Christians don't realize this, but it was this very protest in 1529 at the Council of Spires that earned these German princes the noble name of Protestant.

"The principles contained in this celebrated protest . . . constitute the very essence of Protestantism. Now this protest opposes two abuses of man in matters of faith: the first is the intrusion of the civil magistrate, and the second the arbitrary authority of the church. Instead of these abuses, Protestantism sets the power of the conscience above the magistrate, and the authority of the word of God above the visible church. In the first place, it rejects the civil power in divine things, and says with the prophets and apostles, 'we must obey God rather than man.' In the presence of the crown of Charles the Fifth, it uplifts the crown of Jesus Christ. But it goes farther: it lays down the principle that all human teaching should be subordinate to the oracles of God" (Ibid.).

In essence, this protest placed the Bible above all human traditions, while at the same time it denied the right of any earthly government to enforce religion. The famous Protest of Spires was a protest by Christians against the power of the Roman Catholic Church trying to use the state to control the conscience. This protest defines what it means to be a Protestant. Protestantism stands for freedom. The Bible is above tradition, and religion and big government are to remain separate. This is what Jesus Christ taught when He separated the things of Caesar from the things of God. This is a doctrine of the Lamb, who is gentle, and who never used force.

"Then came the Reformation, protesting against the papal system, and asserting again the rights of the individual conscience, declaring a separation between church and state, and that to Caesar is to be rendered only that which is Caesar's, while men are to be left free to render to God, according to the dictates of their own conscience, that which is God's" (Alonzo T. Jones, *The Two Republics or Rome and the United States of America,* 1891, p. 569).

Are you ready to behold a tremendous truth? This two-fold principle of Jesus Christ, separating the things of Caesar from the things of God, is not only behind the very meaning of the word "Protestant," but it is actually the foundation principle underlying the First Amendment of the Constitution of the United States! "Congress shall make no law" to establish religion. This does not mean that politicians, congressmen, and presidents can't be Christians. It simply means that they are not to use the authority of the government in behalf of their own personal religious ideas. The church is not to control the state nor is the state to control the church. Both are to remain separate and free. This means both civil and religious freedom. These "two" key aspects of our Constitution (civil and religious freedom) are the "two horns like a lamb." Jesus is the Lamb. Lambs are gentle. Jesus does not use force. The Cross itself stands for freedom. Truly, it is the Christian's Statue of Liberty. For over 200 years the Constitution of the United States has maintained this principle. This is one major reason why God has blessed America.

> No one thought of vindicating religion for the conscience of the individual, till a voice from Judea, breaking day for the greatest epoch in the life of humanity, by establishing a pure, spiritual, and universal religion for all mankind, enjoined to render to Caesar only that which is Caesar's. This rule was upheld during the infancy of the gospel for all men. No sooner was the religion adopted by the chief of the Roman empire, than it was shorn of its character of universality, and enthralled by an unholy connection with the unholy state; and so it continued until the new nation,—the least defiled with the barren scoffings of the eighteenth century, the most general believer in Christianity of any people of that age, the chief heir of the Reformation in its purest forms,—when it came to establish a government for the United States. . . .
>
> Vindicating the right of individuality even in religion, and in religion above all,

the new nation dared to set the example of accepting in its relations to God the principle first divinely ordained in Judea. It left the management of temporal things to the temporal power; but the American Constitution, in harmony with the people of the several States, withheld from the Federal government the power to invade the home of reason, the citadel of conscience, the sanctuary of the soul; and not from indifference, but that the infinite Spirit of eternal truth might move in its freedom and purity and power (George Bancroft, *History of the Formation of the Constitution,* book v, ch. i, par. 10, 11).

American democracy with its numerous blessings has its religious origin in a specific Protestant tradition, one that opposed . . . papal supremacy. . . . Its history is closely related to the development of tolerance and religious liberty and the resulting separation of church and state—an ideal that first became translated into reality in the United States of America (V. Norskov Olsen, *Papal Supremacy and American Democracy,* 1987, p. 149).

In the American constitution—a Magna Carta of religious liberty—a New Testament principle and a sixteenth-century ideal became a reality (Ibid., p.150).

> Then came the American Revolution, overturning all the principles of the Papacy, and establishing for the enlightenment of all nations, THE NEW REPUBLIC,—the first national government upon earth that accords with the principles announced by Jesus Christ for mankind and for civil government (Alonzo T. Jones, *The Two Republics or Rome and the United States of America,* 1891, p. 663).

Our founding fathers did not frame the First Amendment of the Bill of Rights to kick God out of America. Hardly! It was because they realized that whenever government unites with religion the result is persecution. It happened in Babylon (read Daniel 3), in Persia (look at Daniel 5), in the Roman Empire (behold the Coliseum), during the Dark Ages (weep over the Inquisition), in England, in many post-Reformation Protestant state churches, and even in colonial America. Finally, after the American Revolution, our new nation was ready for freedom. Not only freedom from the British, but also freedom of and from religion. In the Providence of God, through the influence of men like Roger Williams, Thomas Jefferson, and James Madison, a new constitution was established. A Protestant nation was born. A nation with two horns like a lamb. It is a historical fact that the United States is the first nation in history that has denied the right of government to enforce religion. Why? Because our founding fathers wanted to kick God out of America? No! It was because they did not want to bloody American soil in the name of religion. This had happened in Europe for over a thousand years, and they were sick of it.

What would it take for America to "set up an image" of the Roman Catholic Church? What would have to happen for the United States to become like the Vatican? The answer is simple, yet frightening. The peaceful principle of Jesus Christ, which separates government and religion, would have to be rejected. The Protestant principle of denying the right of religion to use the state to enforce itself would have to be denied. The "two horns like a lamb" would need to become one. Then Protestant America will have formed an image of the Roman Catholic Church.

Prophecy not only predicts that the image will come, but that when it does, it will have "life" (Revelation 13:15). This does not mean that some gigantic idol will someday start breathing and walking around after the Rapture. All of the other beasts in Daniel 7 were alive (Daniel 7:12), which simply means that they were nations of active power. When the image comes to life, this simply means that a new form of this nation has come into existence. The image will then "speak" (Revelation 13:15). This is not referring to some huge, glowing, smoking, and talking statue. What language would it speak anyway? Spanish? No. Nations and kingdoms "speak" by passing laws. The image will "both speak, and cause that as many as would not worship the image of the beast should be killed" (Revelation 13:15). Thus the image will live, speak, and "cause," which implies force. And this use of force will involve worship. Thus, the second beast will enter a new phase and begin passing laws to enforce religion, just like the Roman Catholic Church.

Yet why will such an image be formed and who will do it? The answer to these questions is more amazing than the baptism of a rabbi or the denial of the Virgin Mary by a priest. It will be one of the greatest ironies in all of history. It is with sadness that I write this, but the truth must be told. Do you remember the fall of a number of well-respected TV evangelists? They were Christians, yet they fell from grace. Something similar will occur inside Protestant America during the final moments of time. As the Jewish religious leaders pressured Pontius Pilate, and as the Roman Church united with Constantine and the Roman state, even so will many American Protestants, during a desperate national crisis, finally fall from grace by pressuring our federal government to enforce religion. When religion and government united in Europe, this formed the beast. And during the closing seconds of history, a union of government and religion in America will form the image of the beast. Before this book is over, you will see that all this will happen in the name of Jesus Christ as a supposed solution to our national problems, yet it will deny the Lamb. Why? Because Jesus changes people's lives only through His love, never by force.

Consider this. Not too long ago the front cover of *Time* magazine showed a picture of the cross and the American flag. The headline read: "One Nation Under God—Has the Separation of Church and State Gone Too Far?" The feature article ran this headline: "America's Holy War" (*Time,* Dec. 9, 1991. p. 60). Notice the main issue: "At issue is the meaning of the basic principle enshrined in the First Amendment: that Congress, and by later extension the states, 'shall make no law respecting an establishment of religion, or prohibiting the free exercise thereof.' The modern Supreme Court has taken that to mean that government cannot do anything that promotes either a particular faith or religion in general. The backlash was a long time coming, but now it is here with a vengeance" (Ibid., p. 61).

Do you realize what you just read? That article in *Time* reveals that a reaction is building among Christians in America against the separation of church and state! Near the center of the article was a picture of William Rehnquist, a Lutheran and Antonin Scalia, a Roman Catholic, at a mass in Washington, D.C. In bold letters Rehnquist was quoted as saying, "The wall of separation between church and state is based on bad history. . . . It should be frankly and explicitly abandoned" (Ibid., p. 63). As we have already seen, these words reflect the same Roman Catholic perspective as was expressed in Rome's 1864 *Syllabus of Errors,* and by the letter of Pope Leo XIII in 1888. Yet are you ready for the most amazing thing? William Rehnquist is the Chief Justice of the United States Supreme Court!

Benjamin Franklin wisely declared, "When religion is good, I conceive that it will support itself; and when it does not support itself, and God does not take care to support it, so that its professors are obliged to call for the help of civil powers, 'tis a sign, I apprehend, of it being a bad one." Remember, the early church did not need the help of Caesar. When Christianity has the power of God, it does not need to rely on the power of the state. Yet when it loses this power, it seeks the laws of the government to enforce what it cannot inspire. Thomas Jefferson, the author of the American Declaration of Independence, wrote these memorable words, "It is error alone that needs the support of government. Truth can stand alone." He was right.

American Protestantism is no longer teaching the truth about the Antichrist. Instead, as we have already seen, it is unknowingly and yet forcefully teaching the one-man Antichrist idea of Jesuit futurism, which is actually the very doctrine of the Antichrist. This is why the second beast is finally referred to as "the false prophet" (Revelation 16:13; 19:20). And this gigantic prophetic mistake has also led to a loss of knowledge about the true reasons behind the First Amendment. The truth about the beast and the knowledge that our Bill of Rights was formed against the beast, have all been left behind. There are few protesting Protestants left. And it is these very things that are now contributing to the healing of the deadly wound. I can almost hear Lucifer whispering to his demons, "Everything is going according to our plans."

At 9:02 A.M. on April 19, 1995, the Alfred P. Murrah Federal Building in Oklahoma City was destroyed in the largest terrorist attack in U.S. history. The Oklahoma City National Memorial now stands on the same spot as a sacred monument commemorating the loss of 168 precious lives. Upon entering its large twin-gate frame, visitors can see the cryptic numbers 9:01 on the East Gate and 9:03 on the West Gate. At 9:02, a bomb planted by Timothy McVeigh exploded.

Another 9:02 moment is fast approaching, and when it finally strikes, this world will be plunged into what Daniel called the " 'time of trouble, such as never was since there was a nation' " (Daniel 12:1). During those explosive, closing seconds of history, many Christian leaders, who "know not what they do," will pass over the edge into the abyss of the biggest mistake in history. They will pressure the United States government to enforce religion in a last-ditch effort to save the country. And they will do it in the name of Jesus Christ. This is how the second beast with "two horns like a lamb" will finally "[speak] as a dragon" (Revelation 13:11). This is how Protestant America will form an image of the Roman Catholic Church. And this image will be no fictitious talking statue. It will be real, and we must face it. In a time of desperation, the image will have life, will speak, and will pass a definite law in a misguided attempt to bring America back to God. What kind of a law? After cooperating with the beast and forming his image, the second beast will finally enforce his mark.

CHAPTER

7

Microsoft and the Mark of the Beast

Because the San Andreas fault line runs through the vast city of Los Angeles, those who live in the area are justly concerned about the coming of the "big one"—an earthquake above 7.0. When it comes to apocalyptic issues described in the book of Revelation, the "big one" is definitely the Mark of the Beast. If this subject could be measured by a Richter scale capable of weighing spiritual significance, its magnitude would be well above 1,000. The consequences of receiving the mark are truly catastrophic. Those who get it will experience the wrath of God and lose their souls (Revelation 14:9-11). Therefore nothing could be more serious.

The eighth book in the *Left Behind* drama, *The Mark—The Beast Rules the World,* continues the developing saga of the "Tribulation Force" against the beast after the Rapture. At the height of his sinister reign over mankind, Antichrist Nicolae Carpathia unveils his secret weapon to gain full control of the world—a highly sophisticated "miniature biochip" to be inserted under the skin of people's foreheads and hands "as painlessly as a vaccination in a matter of seconds" (p. 86). "The visible evidence of loyalty to the potentate," this techno-mark also "serves as a method of payment and receipting for buying and selling. Eye-level scanners will allow customers and merchants to merely pass by and be billed or receipted" (pp. 86, 87). This forces Rayford Steele, Buck Williams, and the rest of the Tribulation Force to make a final decision: either submit fully to the Antichrist or expose themselves as Christians. For all who refuse to follow Carpathia, "loyalty enforcement facilitators await with sharpened guillotines" (p. 170).

This incredible scenario reveals what most prophecy-minded Christians today imagine when it comes to the Mark of the Beast. They know it will come from the devil, will be enforced by the Antichrist, will be used to control buying and selling, and they assume it will be centered around some sort of high-tech computer technology. And as we have already seen, the majority also believe it will come after the Rapture. Beyond this, there seems little else to know. Or is there? In this book we have challenged the accuracy of *Left Behind* when it comes to the beast, the image, and the timing of the Rapture. If this blockbuster best-selling series is off track in these key areas, what about its basic theology regarding the Mark of the Beast itself? Is it trustworthy? When it comes to the mark, could *Left Behind* be once again sincerely, yet mistakenly, out in left field?

"And he causeth all, both small and great, rich and poor, free and bond, to receive a mark in their right hand, or in their foreheads" (Revelation 13:16). Here the Bible says a mark will be received in the hand or in the forehead. Yet the Bible does not specifically say it will be a "miniature biochip," or even that it will involve technology at all. These modern words, "computer," "biochip," "technology," "bar code," and "scanner," do not appear in Revelation. People just assume it will happen this way. It's a little bit like the Catholic doctrine of the assumption of the Virgin Mary established in 1950. Because Pope Pius XII proclaimed the assumption to be true, many Catholics now believe Mary was "assumed" or taken to heaven, body and soul, at the end of her earthly life. Yet this is really just a huge "assumption" not supported by the Bible!

Likewise with the Mark of the Beast. Christians assume the mark will involve computer technology developed by a Microsoft or an Intel, yet the Bible itself does not specifically say this. I call this the "Great Mark of the Beast Microchip Assumption."

The Bible specifically does say, "He deceived them that had received the mark of the beast" (Revelation 19:20). Notice carefully. Those who receive the mark are deceived. Therefore the Mark of the Beast must involve some sort of subtle deception. That is, it must not be too obvious or easily noticed. If it were, how could almost the entire world be mislead? Jesus warned us that Satan's deceptions are so tricky they can " 'deceive, if possible, even the elect' " (Matthew 24:24, NKJV).

It seems to me that the *Left Behind* scenario portrays the mass of humankind as altogether too gullible. Think about it. How deceptive would it be for someone like Nicolae Carpathia to command everyone to accept a computerized biochip in their foreheads or in their hands? Honestly, let's get away from fiction and talk about real people. How many real people do you know who would accept big government implanting biochip technology inside their heads? The idea becomes slightly more believable if one imagines a world in which millions of people have just vanished. But what if people don't vanish? What if we are dealing with this world—the real world and real people? Even more than this, what if we are talking about you and me facing the Mark of the Beast? How deceptive would that be to us? How could this "deceive, if possible, even the elect"?

When we look carefully at Revelation, we discover that the Mark of the Beast is not the only thing placed in people's foreheads. Amazingly, the forehead is mentioned many times apart from the mark. The first time the mark is mentioned is in Revelation 13:16. Three verses later John saw a group called the 144,000 with the "Father's name written in their foreheads" (Revelation 14:1). This solitary sentence flashes new light on this whole topic. One group gets the Mark of the Beast while the other group has the name of God in their foreheads. Referring to the saved, the very last chapter of the Bible says, "They shall see his face; and his name shall be in their foreheads" (Revelation 22:4). Therefore, both saints and sinners will all one day have something in their foreheads. Does this mean God's people will walk around with actual, visible letters written on their foreheads?

John also saw an evil scarlet woman riding a beast. "And upon her forehead was a name written, MYSTERY, BABYLON THE GREAT, THE MOTHER OF HARLOTS" (Revelation 17:5). No one doubts this is a symbolic prophecy. There will be no real prostitute riding a beast. Therefore, the writing of that mysterious name upon her forehead must also be symbolic. Are the scales beginning to fall from your eyes? The real issues are more than skin deep.

This idea about the forehead or the hand is not unique to Revelation. Moses told the Israelites, "And these words, which I command thee this day, shall be in thine heart. . . . Thou shalt bind them for a sign on thine hand, and they shall be as frontlets between thine eyes" (Deuteronomy 6:6, 8). Again Moses said, "Therefore shall ye lay up these mine words in your heart and in your soul, and bind them for a sign upon your hand, that they may be as frontlets between your eyes" (Deuteronomy 11:18). What did God intend the Israelites to learn from this? Did the Lord want them to take a fine-point pen and write a whole lot of words on the tiny bit of skin between their eyes above their noses? How could their faces contain the entire book of Deuteronomy? It has thirty-four chapters!

With a little bit of reflection we should be able to understand what this idea of the forehead and hand is really all about. Anciently, God wanted His words on the foreheads of the Israelites. This must mean He wanted them inside of their minds. What about His words on their hands? This must apply to their actions. So, the forehead represents the mind, and the hand represents the actions. That's simple enough. Therefore, what the book of Revelation is really saying when it speaks of a mark in the forehead or in the hand is that one day the masses of humanity will fully yield their minds and their actions to some specific idea, or tradition, or "mark" that comes from the beast. They will be marked in their minds. Yet God's true people will see through this deception. Why? Because they have the name of God in their foreheads.

What is the name of God? Is it only a specific set of syllables God would like us to use when we address Him, or does this issue involve more than mere pronunciation? When Moses ascended Mount Sinai, "The LORD descended in the cloud, and stood with him there, and proclaimed the name of the LORD" (Exodus 34:5). Then God described His character. He revealed Himself as merciful, gracious, patient, forgiving, just, and full of truth (Exodus 34:6, 7). These wonderful attributes are referred to as "the name of the LORD." At the end of His earthly life, in a prayer to His Father, our Savior said, "I have manifested thy name unto the men which thou gavest me out of the world" (John 17:6). Jesus didn't say this simply because He had been pronouncing certain syllables correctly, but because His life revealed the true character of God. So when the Bible says people will have the name of God on their foreheads, this means that His gracious attributes of character have become a deep part of their thinking and actions. They are truly connected with Jesus Christ. In the final days, God will have a people who are so firmly rooted in Jesus and in His attributes of character that they will not be deceived or go along with the Mark of the Beast. Thus, we are dealing with deep spiritual issues.

The mark is mentioned eight times in Revelation (13:16, 17; 14:9, 11; 15:2; 16: 2; 19:20; 20:4), but there is only one unique section that specifically and comprehensively clarifies the issues and warns the entire world against receiving this evil mark. It is the three angels' messages found in Revelation 14:6-12. Sadly, most Christians have never even heard of these messages, yet they are of cosmic significance. They are just as important as the message of Noah before the Flood. Why? Because they contain Heaven's last call before the return of Jesus Christ (Revelation 14:14-16).

John saw the first "angel flying in the midst of heaven," followed by "another angel," and then by a "third angel" (Revelation 14:6, 8, 9). All three of these angels have tremendous things to say "to those who dwell on the earth—to every nation, tribe, tongue, and people" (Revelation 14:6, NKJV). This does not mean that literal angels will appear in the sky flying over Los Angeles, New York, Tokyo, Paris, London, and Moscow. As with many other things in Revelation, these angels are symbolic. They represent a final group of Christians who proclaim God's last message to the whole world from the pulpit, on the radio, on television, in print, and via satellite. Instead of the fictitious "Tribulation Force," we might call them God's real "Three Angels' Messages Force." They expose the real Antichrist, counteract the tidal wave of Jesuit futurism, and teach the actual truth about Satan's evil mark.

Here's a quick overview of these mighty messages. The first angel proclaims the everlasting gospel of Jesus Christ, the hour of judgment, and the importance of worshiping the Creator of heaven and earth (Revelation 14:6, 7). The second angel announces the fall of the Babylonian harlot, which has made the whole earth drunk with her confusing wine of deception (Revelation 14:8). The third angel solemnly warns about the beast, the image, and the deadly mark, stating that those who receive the mark will drink the wine of the wrath of God (Revelation 14:10, 11). The third angel concludes with these highly significant words, "Here is the patience of the saints: here are they that keep the commandments of God, and the faith of Jesus" (Revelation 14:12). As soon as God's real "Three Angels' Messages Force" has completed its heavenly assignment, there follows a power-packed description of the return of Jesus Christ on a white cloud to reap the final harvest of the earth (Revelation 14:14-16).

Let's unpack these mighty issues, beginning with the all-important topic of worshiping the Creator. The first angel says with a loud voice, "Worship him that made heaven, and earth, and the sea, and the fountains of waters" (Revelation 14:7). Then the third angel thunders, "If any man worship the beast and his image, and receive his mark in his forehead or in his hand, the same shall drink of the wine of the wrath of God" (Revelation 14:9, 10). Here people are given the ultimate choice: Either worship the Creator or worship the beast and receive his mark. Thus, the issue of worshiping the Creator is central to avoiding the mark.

The next mighty issue is one few people are aware of. Most best-selling prophecy books and blockbuster Tribulation movies skip right over it. Those who believe the mark is a biochip developed by some high-tech firm like Microsoft or Intel usually miss it entirely. As we have already seen, immediately after the third angel warns humankind about receiving the mark, the very next sentence says, "Here is the patience of the saints: here are they that keep the commandments of God, and the faith of Jesus" (Revelation 14:12). Here one group receives the mark, while the other group "keeps the commandments of God and the faith of Jesus." Thus, the issue of keeping the commandments of God is also central to avoiding the mark. In a little while we will place this hidden issue fully under the microscope.

Have you heard of a brand of toothpaste called "Close-Up"? It is designed to make one's breath smell sweet. When we take a "Close-Up" look at the three angels' messages, we discover that the sweetest part of all has to do with a Person, the person of Jesus Christ. The first angel announces to the world "the everlasting gospel" (Revelation 14:6), which literally means the good news of Jesus Christ. The third angel speaks of "the Lamb" in contrast with the beast (Revelation 14:9, 10), which is another reference to Jesus Christ, pointing to His unfathomable love and sacrifice on the cross. And the very last word of the third angel's message is "Jesus" (Revelation 14:12). Thus, we discover a laser-like focus on "the gospel," the "Lamb," and on "Jesus" Himself. To summarize thus far: Those who believe in Jesus Christ, accept the gospel, follow the Lamb, worship the Creator, and keep the commandments of God—these will not worship the beast and receive his mark. Like the unparalleled majesty of Mount Everest, these mighty issues regarding the Mark of the Beast are now rising up before our very eyes.

Jesus Christ is center stage, and so is the worship of the Creator. Once again, let's take a closer look. The first angel says, "Worship him that made heaven, and earth" (Revelation 14:7), but who is the Maker of heaven and earth? What does the New Testament really say? Speaking of Jesus Christ, the Bible says, "He was in the world, and the world was made by him, and the world knew him not" (John 1:10). Do you see it? John is saying that the One who was in the world is also the very One who made the world. Those in John's time didn't understand this, and neither do most people today. Yet the Bible is telling us that Jesus Christ is not only our Savior, but He is also the Maker of planet Earth. That humble Man who walked our dusty roads, who ate our food, who slept outside under our stars, and who spoke words of love to those who were just plain stressed out, is actually the great Creator of all life.

Jesus Christ is "The Word." We know this because John wrote, "The Word was made flesh, and dwelt among us" (John 1:14). These words reveal that Jesus did not begin His life in a manger, but that He existed long before He became a tiny baby inside of Mary. Speaking of the One to be born in Bethlehem, an ancient prophet wrote, "Whose goings forth have been from of old, from everlasting" (Micah 5:2). Thus, the Baby of Bethlehem is an eternal Being who existed long before the time of Joseph, Herod, and the wise men.

The very first words in the book of John reveal, "In the beginning was the Word, and the Word was with God, and the Word was God. The same was in the beginning with God. All things were made by him; and without him was not anything made that was made" (John 1:1-3). Once again the wonderful and beautiful truth is established that Jesus is the Maker of everything. Nothing exists apart from Him. He made Adam and Eve, the mountains and the trees, the sun, moon and stars, all of the animals, every shiny fish, and your favorite pet.

"For by him were all things created, that are in heaven, and that are in earth, visible and invisible, whether they be thrones, or dominions, or principalities, or powers: all things were created by him, and for him: And he is before all things, and by him all things consist" (Colossians 1:16, 17). Let this thought both amaze and subdue us; the Eternal One who made this earth is the very One who died almost naked on a splintered cross in the Middle East. "In whom we have redemption through his blood, even the forgiveness of sins" (Colossians 1:14). When we fully yield to God's love, say "Goodbye" to every sin, stop trusting in ourselves, and start really believing in Jesus Christ, our merciful heavenly Father will forgive us, and grant us the free gift of eternal life (see Ephesians 2:8; 1 Corinthians 15:3; Acts 20:21; and 1 John 1:9). This good news is called "the everlasting gospel" in the first angel's message.

Therefore, when the first angel tells everyone to "worship him that made heaven, and earth, and the sea, and the fountains of waters" (Revelation 14:7), this is a special end-time call to worship Jesus Christ, not only as Savior, but also specifically as the Maker of all life. And amazingly, this very issue is closely tied in with the Mark of the Beast, for we have already discovered that those who worship the Creator are placed in contrast with those who worship the beast and receive his mark. Yet what exactly is the Mark of the Beast? Is it possible to know for sure without indulging in wild-eyed speculation? I believe it is. We still have a few more pieces to put together in this awesome prophetic puzzle, yet when we are finished, it will become extremely clear what the Mark of the Beast is. In fact, there will be no mistaking it.

In some Hollywood action movies, a high-impact "red button" is finally pushed inside some technological control center. In a symbolic sense, it's time for us to push a "red button" of deep prophetic insight. Here goes. The deadly mark is the Mark of the Beast; it's a mark that comes from the beast itself. John saw those who gained "the victory over the beast, and over his image, and over his mark" (Revelation 15:2). Logic tells us that in order to understand "his mark," we must correctly interpret who "he" is. Who is this beast? Some think the beast is a huge computer in Belgium. The *Left Behind* novels portray the beast as a super-powerful, devil-indwelt Romanian who gains control of the world after the Rapture. Yet what have we learned in this book? Who did Martin Luther, John Calvin, John Wesley, the translators of the King James Bible, Sir Isaac Newton, Charles Spurgeon, and countless other historic Protestants think the beast was? What power arose out of the Roman Empire, has spoken great words against God, has made war on the saints, has received a deadly wound which is now healing, and has fulfilled every point of this prophecy? Now you know the answer. It is the Roman Catholic Church. And the mark is "his mark." Therefore the Mark of the Beast must be something that comes from the Roman Catholic Church itself.

Not long ago someone handed me a copy of a very old Bible from the 1800s that had belonged to a Presbyterian lay pastor. Certain texts throughout this Bible contain footnotes reflecting the beliefs of Christians in the nineteenth century. I quickly turned to Revelation 13:16 about the Mark of the Beast, and I discovered footnotes that would probably not appear in a Scofield Reference Bible. I was stunned when I read: "Ver. 16. A mark. Submission to the rites and ceremonies of the papal communion. In their right hand. By active obedience to the papal power. Or in their foreheads. By outward profession of its doctrines and infallible authority" (*The New Testament: With Commentaries, References, Harmony of the Gospels and the Helps Needed to Understand and Teach the Text.* 1895. New York and St. Louis. N.D. Thompson Pub. Co., p. 530). When those words were written, Bill Gates wasn't born yet, nor was there a company called Microsoft. In the footnotes of that Bible, when it came to the Mark of the Beast, computer technology was a non-issue. What mattered was submission or resistance to the Roman Catholic Church!

The third angel's message is now crying out with a loud voice to everyone, "If anyman worship the beast and his image, and receive his mark in his forehead, or in his hand, the same shall drink of the wine of the wrath of God" (Revelation 14:9, 10). Now think about it. Would Jesus tell us in Revelation, "The mark is coming, so watch out. It will be tricky, almost deceiving the very elect. I love you, and died for you, yet I can't tell you exactly what this mysterious mark is. If you get it, you'll be lost. You're on your own." Does this sound logical? Would Jesus show and not tell? Why would God send a message to the whole world about the mark, and then keep its identity a secret? How could such a message be given with a loud voice? Imagine Noah preaching, "Quick! Get into the ark, because the Flood is coming! That is, I'm pretty sure, although I'm not entirely positive." Impossible! It is the same with the third angel's message. Again, think about it. Can we know for sure who the beast is? Yes. Therefore, we must be able to find out from the Bible itself exactly what the mark is. Logic, reason, and the integrity of God's loving character require this.

We are about to make another amazing discovery. Remember those X-ray eyeglasses I talked about in chapter 3 of this book? Well, there is a certain X-ray text in the Bible that will, if we let it, supernaturally enable us to see exactly what the Mark of the Beast is. I also call it our golden clue. We can find it by carefully comparing Revelation 13 with its Old Testament counterpart, Daniel 7. These two chapters fit together like a key fits into a lock. The connections are easily seen. Both chapters talk about beasts from the sea, a lion, a bear, a leopard, a dragon, ten horns, a mouth speaking great things, war on the saints, and a specific time period of three and a half years or forty-two months. Interpretations may vary, but almost all Protestant, Catholic, and Evangelical scholars, including the authors of *Left Behind,* agree that the little horn of Daniel 7 and the first beast of Revelation 13 refer to the same thing—the Antichrist. Yet there is something many people have missed that is right there in God's Word. And not only does it tie in with the Mark of the Beast but, it is a golden clue as to what the mark really is.

The very first time the Mark of the Beast is mentioned in the Bible is near the end of Revelation 13. Now, if other aspects of the beast in Revelation 13 find such a perfect parallel in the little horn of Daniel 7, then what about the mark? Could there be something near the end of Daniel 7 that parallels the mark near the end of Revelation 13? Yes, there is. It is in verse 25. Daniel 7:25 says the little horn will speak great words against God, and this idea is also found in Revelation 13:5. Daniel 7:25 says he will wear out, or make war, on the saints, and this idea is also found in Revelation 13:7. Daniel 7:25 says the horn will rule for three and a half years, and this point is also restated in Revelation 13:5. Thus, every point of Daniel 7:25 finds a perfect parallel in Revelation 13. Yet there is one point in Daniel 7:25 we have not yet touched upon. Most people miss it, few ever explain it, yet there it is. It is our golden clue. You may not believe this, but the final destiny of the world is connected with it.

Are you ready? Here it is. The little horn will also "think to change times and laws" (Daniel

7:25). What does this mysterious sentence mean? Most have no idea. Notice that little word "change." The horn will "change" something, then the beast will enforce his mark. Could this change, whatever it is, be connected with the mark? Let's think about it. Can a change be a mark? Has anyone ever entered your life and changed you so deeply that it can truly be said, "He left his mark?" Imagine a man losing his temper and punching another man in the eye. What would show up around that eye the next day? A mark. What if a vandal entered your home and hit your computer screen with a hammer, changing its surface? The next day, as you surveyed your shattered monitor, you could plainly see where that man had left his terrible mark.

Yet what exactly will the little horn think to change? He shall "think to change times and laws" (Daniel 7:25). Because the Antichrist comes during New Testament times, it is evident that some of God's "laws" must still exist this side of the Cross. When Jesus died, He put an end to the sacrificial laws of the Old Testament, which pointed forward to His death, and this is why we no longer sacrifice lambs. Those laws are gone. Yet what about the Ten Commandments? Do they still apply to us?

Let's have a brief Bible study on law and grace. An essential part of "the everlasting gospel" of the first angel's message is the truth that Christians are "justified by faith apart from the deeds of the law" (Romans 3:28, NKJV). Paul wrote: "By grace are ye saved through faith; and that not of yourselves: it is the gift of God: Not of works, lest any man should boast" (Ephesians 2:8, 9). This mighty New Testament truth became one of the battle cries of the Protestant Reformation. Martin Luther boldly taught that a person is saved through repentance and faith in Jesus Christ, rather than through pilgrimages, idol worship, prayers to Mary, confessions to a priest, or any other human work. Renouncing self and all self-merits, we are to trust completely in the merits and worthiness of Jesus alone. Yet the Roman Church could not accept this. This led to the great divorce.

The Bible urges us to "Behold the lamb of God, which taketh away the sin of the world" (John 1:29). The more we discover who Jesus Christ is, how much He loves us, and how He died on a cruel cross for all of our sins, the more we are drawn to God. We see Him in His true character of love and friendliness. "Christ died for our sins according to the scriptures" (1 Corinthians 15:3). The Bible teaches, "repentance toward God, and faith toward our Lord Jesus Christ" (Acts 20:21). "If we confess our sins, he is faithful and just to forgive us our sins, and to cleanse us from all unrighteousness" (1 John 1:9). Jesus said, "This is my blood of the new testament, which is shed for many for the remission of sins" (Matthew 26:28). Through repentance and faith in the dripping blood of the Lamb, we are forgiven and accepted by God just as if we had never sinned. "All that believe are justified" (Acts 13:39). This is what the Bible calls, "good news." Jesus has already died for us, paid for our sins, and His free salvation is now offered to us all.

This good news is also powerful news to transform our lives. When a person surrenders fully to Jesus Christ, he is born again. The Holy Spirit enters the life and changes the heart. Peter said, "Ye shall receive the gift of the Holy Ghost" (Acts 2:38). Believers receive a divine power that begins to work on the inside. Then how should a Christian, saved by grace, relate to God's law? After describing salvation by grace apart from works in Ephesians 2:8, 9, the same Paul wrote in the same book, "Children, obey your parents in the Lord: for this is right. Honor thy father and mother; which is the first commandment with promise" (Ephesians 6:1, 2). "Honour thy father and thy mother" is the fifth commandment (Exodus 20:12). In the same book, Paul also wrote, "Let him that stole steal no more" (Ephesians 4:28). "Thou shalt not steal" is the eighth commandment (Exodus 20:15).

James also wrote, "He that said, Do not commit adultery, said also, Do not kill. Now, if thou commit no adultery, yet if thou kill, thou art become a transgressor of the law" (James 2:11). Here, James tells Christians to keep the sixth and seventh commandments. Jesus Himself said, "It is easier for heaven and earth to pass, than one tittle of the law to fail. Whosoever putteth away his wife, and marries another, committeth adultery" (Luke 16:17, 18). Thus, Jesus upheld the seventh commandment. Near the end of His earthly life, in touching tones of love, Jesus Christ appealed to His followers, "If you love me, keep my commandments" (John 14:15). These words are actually a quote from the second commandment, which states, "Shewing mercy unto thousands of them that love me, and keep my commandments" (Exodus 20:6). Thus, the New Testament is very clear—Christians who are saved by grace should also love Jesus Christ and keep the Ten Commandments, through the power of the Holy Spirit. Who can truly disagree with that?

What does all of this have to do with the Mark of the Beast? You are about to find out. First, let me summarize some major points. Just as there are ten commandments, even so there are ten fundamental facts in our Bibles about the Mark of the Beast. These facts do not represent *Left Behind* fiction, but real truths found in God's Word:

1. The Mark of the Beast is deceptive, not obvious (Revelation 19:20).
2. The mark will be received on the forehead, which represents the mind, or on the hand, which represents the actions (Revelation 14:9; Deuteronomy 11:18).

3. The three angels reveal a comprehensive message from God before the Second Coming of Jesus Christ to all the world to help people understand the mark (Revelation 14:6-16).
4. Those who worship Jesus Christ as Creator will not get the mark (Revelation 14:7, 9-11; John 1:3, 10).
5. Those who keep the Ten Commandments will not get the mark (Revelation 14:9, 12).
6. The mark comes from the beast, which represents the Roman Catholic Church.
7. The warning against the mark will be given with a loud voice, thus it must be clear and easy to understand (Revelation 14:9).
8. The mark involves a special sin against God Himself, for those who receive it will drink the wine of His wrath (Revelation 14:9, 10).
9. The mark has something to do with the changing of God's law (compare Daniel 7:25 with Revelation 13:16).
10. The Mark of the Beast has something to do with the changing of the times and laws of God (Daniel 7:25).

Let's take a look again at our little-known, golden-clue text, He shall "think to change times and laws" (Daniel 7:25). Now notice that word, "times." We know the word "laws" has to do with the Ten Commandments, which continue after the Cross. But what about "times"? OK, here we go. We are almost at the bottom line. You are about to discover something you will hardly believe. It's a truth so shocking it can hardly be written. It shatters all false interpretations, which may sincerely, yet deceptively, hide the real issues. If you pray and humbly study this out, you will know for sure it's true. Are you ready? There is only one of the Ten Commandments that has to do with "time." There is only one that has to do with the Creator of heaven and earth. And this single, solitary commandment is the only one of the Ten Commandments that the Roman Catholic Church specifically says it has changed. It is the commandment that says, "Remember the Sabbath day, to keep it holy" (Exodus 20:8)—the commandment that points to Jesus Christ as the Maker of all life.

Before we go any further, I want to share with you a very important thought. The Bible says, "But thou, O Daniel, shut up the words, and seal the book, even to the time of the end: many shall run to and fro, and knowledge shall be increased" (Daniel 12:4). This verse tells us that in the final times, God will be giving new light to His people. This especially applies to an increase of knowledge of the book of Daniel, which includes our golden-clue text: He shall "think to change times and laws" (Daniel 7:25). In the final days, God will help His people understand what this changing of "times" is really all about. This doesn't mean that previous generations of godly Christians who never had this special end-time light are lost. Nor does it mean that believers today who haven't yet grasped it are doomed. But it does mean that God has new light for this final generation. Thus, we need a certain openness of mind to learn something new. Someone once said, "The purpose of an open mind is to close it on the truth." So let's be open, testing everything by Scripture.

God Almighty did not write the ten suggestions, but the Ten Commandments. The fourth says, "Remember the Sabbath day, to keep it holy. Six days shalt thou labour, and do all thy work: But the seventh day is the sabbath of the Lord thy God: in it thou shalt not do any work, . . . For in six days the LORD made heaven and earth, the sea, and all that in them is, and rested the seventh day: wherefore the LORD blessed the sabbath day, and hallowed it" (Exodus 20:8-11).

"Remember the sabbath day, to keep it holy." Where do we remember? In our foreheads. "Six days shalt thou labour, and do all thy work: But the seventh day is the sabbath of the Lord thy God: in it thou shalt not do any work." With what do we work? With our hands. Thus, the Sabbath commandment deals with both the forehead and the hand. The "seventh day" is specified as "the Sabbath of the Lord." It is not the Sabbath of the Jews, but of the Lord. "For in six days the LORD made heaven and earth, the sea, and all that in them is, and rested the seventh day." These words are directly quoted in the first angel's message (see Revelation 14:7). And who is this "Lord" that "made heaven and earth"? As we have already seen, according to the New Testament, it is Jesus Christ. Thus, the Sabbath commandment, in a unique and special sense, reveals Jesus Christ as Lord and as the Maker of all life.

A well-known Roman Catholic catechism declares:

> Q. Which is the Sabbath day? A. Saturday is the Sabbath day. Q. Why do we observe Sunday instead of Saturday? Answer: We observe Sunday instead of Saturday because the Catholic Church transferred the solemnity from Saturday to Sunday (*The Converts Catechism of Catholic Doctrine,* by Peter Geiermann, 1946, p. 50).

> The Catholic Church for over one thousand years before the existence of a Protestant, by virtue of her divine mission, changed the day from Saturday to Sunday (*The Christian Sabbath,* p. 29. Printed by The Catholic Mirror, the official organ of Cardinal Gibbons, Baltimore, Md., 1893).

> The Pope is of so great authority and

> power that he can modify, change, or interpret even divine laws (Farraris's *Ecclesiastical Dictionary.* Article, "The Pope").

> Of course the change [from Sabbath to Sunday] was her act . . . and the act is a mark of her ecclesiastical power and authority in religious matters (Signed by H. F. Thomas, Chancellor for Cardinal Gibbons, in a letter dated, Nov. 11, 1895).

Thus, the Catholic Church claims the pope has power to change God's law, just as Daniel 7:25 says. This church claims to have changed the Sabbath into Sunday, which is a changing of "times," just as Daniel 7:25 says will occur. And papal Rome also calls this change a "mark" of her authority, which makes this a perfect fit with Revelation 13!

This issue of Sabbath or Sunday is now the hottest, most intense, and most explosive issue facing the Christian world. An entire book could be written on this subject alone. It is outside the scope of *Truth Left Behind* to deal with every single argument for or against Sabbath keeping, yet we will address the major issues. Let's start by looking at ten key Sunday facts found in the New Testament:

1. Jesus Christ rose on Sunday, "the first day of the week" (Mark 16:9).
2. The New Testament refers to "the first day

of the week" eight times (Matthew 28:1; Mark 16:1, 9; Luke 24:1; John 20:1, 19; 1 Corinthians 16:1; Acts 20:7).

3. Five of these references are about the Resurrection (Matthew 28:1; Mark 16:1, 9; Luke 24:1; John 20:1).
4. One Sunday text refers to a fearful gathering of the disciples on that day before they knew Jesus was alive (John 20:19).
5. One Sunday text refers to a special collection of money on that day in the city of Corinth for a group of poor believers in Jerusalem (1 Corinthians 16:1-3; Romans 15:25, 26).
6. And one text refers to a solitary instance in Troas where believers gathered late one Saturday night as a farewell to Paul (Acts 20:6-13).
7. None of these references even remotely suggest that Sunday is now holy or that it has been set aside in honor of the Resurrection.
8. Jesus Christ never said a word about Sunday in any of His teachings.
9. Jesus Christ gave His church authority to teach only what He taught (Matthew 28:19), which forbids any emphasis on Sunday keeping.
10. The New Testament is as silent as a cemetery about any change from Sabbath to Sunday.

By way of contrast, here are ten key Sabbath facts found in your own Bible:

1. Jesus Christ kept the Sabbath (Luke 4:16).
2. Jesus taught much about the Sabbath (Matthew 12:1-14).
3. Jesus said He is "Lord of the Sabbath," thus revealing that it is His own special day in honor of the fact that He is the Creator of all life (Mark 2:28; Matthew 12:8).
4. Jesus often healed people on the Sabbath, revealing His love and power (Matthew 12:9-13).
5. Jesus freed the Sabbath from the burdensome traditions of the Pharisees (Luke 13:10-17).
6. The Sabbath was kept by Christ's disciples after the Cross (Luke 23:46, 54-56).
7. The Sabbath was kept in the book of Acts by both Jews and Gentiles (Acts 13:42-44; 16:13; 17:1-4; 18:4).
8. The entire book of Revelation was given "on the Lord's day" which is the Sabbath day (Revelation 1:10; Exodus 20:10; Isaiah 58:13; Matthew 12:8).
9. The Sabbath is not just for Jews, but is also for Gentiles (Isaiah 56:1-8).
10. The Sabbath will be kept in the new earth by all the saved (Isaiah 66:22, 23).

In the next few paragraphs I am going to get

very specific about certain arguments which I have heard against this "new light" about keeping the Sabbath. Some of this may seem a bit technical, yet it is necessary to cover this subject thoroughly. As I go through these arguments, it is not my purpose to attack other Christians. Yet in the interest of truth, we must carefully study the Word of God. We need to look at this topic from every possible angle.

I have spoken about this hot subject in cities across America, and in my many discussions with Christians, I have discovered that, just as there was a Roman Catholic counter Reformation, so there are two major counter texts now being used against Sabbath keeping. The first is Romans 14:5, 6 where Paul talks about eating or not eating certain things, and esteeming or not esteeming certain days. Many people apply this to the Sabbath, but this is a mistake. When we carefully compare Romans 14 with 1 Corinthians 8, we learn that Paul was referring to eating or not eating food sacrificed to idols on certain pagan feast days. He may also have been thinking about certain Jewish feasts or fast days (see Luke 18:12). The very first verse of Romans 14 tells us that this chapter is dealing with "doubtful disputations" (KJV) or "disputes over doubtful things" (NKJV). Thus, Romans 14 is not a discussion of the Ten Commandments, which are not "doubtful," but exceedingly clear, "written with the finger of God"(Exodus 31:18). In any case, Romans 14 says nothing about the Sabbath.

The second major counter text now being used against the Sabbath is Colossians 2:16. But when we look at its context, we discover something that is often overlooked. Jesus Christ, "blott[ed] out the handwriting of ordinances that was against us . . . nailing it to his cross" (2:14). The "handwriting of ordinances" was not the Ten Commandments, which were not written by any human hand, but with the finger of God (Exodus 31:18). It was the ceremonial law that was written with the hand of Moses (Deuteronomy 31:24-26). It was this "handwriting of ordinances" that was nailed to the cross. Paul continued, "Let no man therefore judge you in meat, or in drink, or in respect of an holyday, or of the new moon, or of the sabbath days: Which are a shadow of things to come" (Colossians 2:16, 17). People sometimes apply those "sabbath days" in verse 16 to the Creation Sabbath of the Ten Commandments, yet again, this is a mistake. Paul is referring to the meat offerings, drink offerings, and the yearly sabbaths of the ceremonial law (Leviticus 23:24, 27, 32, 37-39), not the Sabbath of the fourth commandment. The yearly ceremonial sabbaths (Passover, Day of Atonement, etc.) were shadows pointing forward to Jesus Christ (see Hebrews 10:1). The Creation Sabbath is not a shadow, for it points *back* to the beginning of the world (Exodus 20:11)! Along with the other nine commandments, it was definitely not nailed to the cross (Revelation 11:19; 12:17; 14:12).

Some say, "We keep Sunday because we are under the new covenant." Yet it is impossible for Sunday to be part of the new covenant because Sunday came *after* Jesus Christ died! It was His death that "confirmed" the covenant. Paul said that after a covenant is confirmed by death, "no man disannulleth or addeth thereto" (Galatians 3:15). Some say, "Sabbath keeping is legalism," yet they would not say this about such commands as "Honor your father and mother" or "Do not commit adultery" or "Do not steal." So why make that charge against Sabbath keeping? Besides, this is the only commandment of the ten in which God specifically said, "Remember"! Should we forget the only one God said not to? Some are too willing to abolish the whole ten-commandment law just to get around the fourth one. Yet this is very strange, especially at a time when Christians everywhere would like to see the Ten Commandments hanging once again on the walls of our public schools.

Others say, "If Christians are supposed to keep the Sabbath, why are all of the other Ten Commandments carried over into the New Testament, except the fourth?" Yet the fourth *is* in the New Testament! The Bible says that after Jesus died, His followers "rested the Sabbath day according to the commandment" (Luke 23:56). There it is. The "commandment" was still there after the Cross, and Luke wrote this about twenty-eight years after the Resurrection.

Still others object, "But we are not under the law; we are under grace!" quoting Romans 6:14. This is true, yet people fail to read the very next verse. Paul continued: "What then? shall we sin, because we are not under the law, but under grace? God forbid" (6:15). What is sin? "Sin is the transgression of the law" (1 John 3:4). Simply put the pieces together. Even though we are under grace, this does not mean we are free to break any one of the Ten Commandments. If we may disregard the fourth commandment, why can we not also disregard the other nine?

The most common argument is, "We keep Sunday in honor of the Resurrection." But the Bible nowhere supports this. The truth is, *baptism* commemorates the death, burial, and resurrection of Jesus Christ (Romans 6:4). Besides, how could the Resurrection change one of the Ten Commandments? Shall we use the resurrection of Jesus Christ on Sunday as a reason to break the law of God, which says, "Remember the sabbath day, to keep it holy" (Exodus 20:8)? Paul asked, "Is therefore Christ the minister of sin? God forbid" (Galatians 2:17). It's true that Paul taught that we are not saved or justified by the law, but by the grace of Jesus Christ (Romans 3:28). This is a Protestant principle. But then Paul asked, "Do we then make void the law through faith? God forbid: yea, we establish the law" (Romans 3:31).

The Catholic Council of Trent said tradition

is equal with Scripture. Yet Protestants responded, "No way! The Bible is above tradition!" This is another major Protestant principle. Dear friend, Sunday is only a tradition of men. Shall we follow the Bible or tradition?

Others ask, "Then why didn't the Reformers keep the Sabbath?" The reason is simple. They were just coming out of the midnight blackness of the Dark Ages, and they could handle only so much light. Jesus said, "I have yet many things to say unto you, but you cannot bear them now" (John 16:12). Yet we live in the final days. The Bible says, "But thou, O Daniel, shut up the words, and seal the book, even to the time of the end: many shall run to and fro, and knowledge shall be increased" (Daniel 12:4). Knowledge is increasing, and fuller light now shines. This especially applies to our golden-clue text: He shall "think to change times and laws" (Daniel 7:25). This is no minor matter, for we are talking about one of the Ten Commandments that the Almighty God wrote with His own all-powerful finger on two tables of stone (Exodus 31:18). Have you ever heard anyone say, "We can change this or that because it is not written in stone?" Friend, stone is stone, and rock is rock. There is simply no use in beating our heads against this truth. God's law has not changed! Read Matthew 5:17-19.

Did you hear about the high-tech hackers who illegally emailed their way into Microsoft's internal corporate network in November 2000?

Microsoft's public relations spinners insisted that the intruders did not view or alter any of Microsoft's source code, yet Bill Gates was very concerned that his enemies "could have built secret 'back doors' into future programs, ensuring access to computers worldwide" (*Newsweek,* Nov. 6, 2000, p. 8). This was an attack on the source code of the world's largest software maker. The Bible also describes an illegal attack upon the "source code" of the great King of the universe. The little horn has "[changed] times and laws" (Daniel 7:25). It has hacked its way into the very heart of the Ten Commandments, the foundation of God's government in heaven and earth. It has altered the Bible Sabbath of Jesus Christ from Saturday to Sunday, and now it claims that Sunday is a mark of its authority as the true church. Thus, Rome admits what prophecy predicts. The pieces fit together too perfectly for us to doubt. According to the Bible and the Roman Church itself, Sunday is the Mark of the Beast.

Yet I want to clarify something of the utmost importance. No one has this mark right now. Most Christians have never really studied this subject before. There are true Christians in all churches, including the Roman Catholic Church. Yes, God has sincere people everywhere. Yet one of these days, according to the book of Revelation, this mark of Rome's authority will be enforced by law around the world. Then, after people's minds have been enlightened, the final time of choice will come.

The Bible says, "He causeth all, both small and great, rich and poor, free and bond, to receive a mark in their right hand, or in their foreheads: And that no man might buy or sell, save he that had the mark" (Revelation 13:16, 17). Thus, this mark of Rome's authority is destined to be enforced by law. This may shock you, but Sunday laws have been enforced in various degrees for 1,700 years. The first Sunday law was enforced by the Roman emperor Constantine on March 7, A.D. 321. His famous edict declared, "On the venerable day of the sun [Sunday] let the magistrates and people residing in the cities rest, and let all workshops be closed" (Schaff's translation, *History of the Christian Church,* vol. iii, p. 75. See also the Code of Justinian, Book 3, Title 12, Law 3).

Why did Constantine pass this Sunday law? The reasons are both fascinating and relevant for us today. In the fourth century, the Roman Empire was disintegrating. Morality was at an all-time low. Yet religion was far from dead. Constantine himself was a dedicated sun-worshiper, as were the majority of his subjects. In fact, the very name "Sunday" stems from pagan sun worship. By this time, a growing number of Christians were following the Catholic Church's example of giving up the Sabbath and keeping Sunday in honor of the Resurrection. Constantine had already seen the moral strength of Christianity as revealed in the courage of its martyrs, and this gave him an idea. He thought to himself, "Why not unite the Christians and the pagans together through their mutual respect for Sunday?" That's why he passed his famous Sunday law hoping to bring unity into his empire, thus saving it from ruin. His plan failed, and Rome still went down.

Constantine's Sunday law "was his mode of harmonizing the Christian and Pagan elements of the empire under one common institution" (A. P. Stanley, *Lectures on the History of the Eastern Church*, p. 227. 1861). But he went further than this. He not only claimed to become a Christian himself, but he also favored the Roman Catholic Church. Through Constantine's influence, the Catholic Church's political power grew strong. A union between the Catholic Church and Constantine's state developed. Yet Constantine really remained a pagan at heart. "His coins bore on the one side the letters of the name of Christ; on the other the figures of the Sun-god" (Ibid.) Thus, Constantine contributed to the uniting of the Roman Catholic Church with the Roman state and to the forming of the beast, and it happened through the enforcement of Sunday.

After Constantine, the Roman Catholic Church continued to enforce the keeping of Sunday in Europe for over 1,000 years. Sunday laws were also enforced in England for centuries. Amazingly, this practice was continued in colonial America. I have in my library a book, *Dateline Sunday, USA—The Story of Three and a Half*

Centuries of Sunday-law Battles in America, written by Attorney Warren L. Johns (1967). This book reveals that in spite of the desire of the early American Puritans to get away from everything Catholic, they still maintained the keeping of Sunday and even the enforcement of Sunday laws. In the 1600s, if you lived in Massachusetts, Virginia, or Connecticut, you were required by law to attend church on Sunday. Disobedience was punished by heavy fines, whipping, confinement in a cage, and in some cases, even by death. Thus, colonial Protestant America still followed the example of Constantine and the Catholic Church in the uniting of church and state, and in the enforcement of Sunday laws.

The American Revolution resulted in complete separation from England and in the forming of a new nation. The American Constitution and the Bill of Rights fully established the doctrine of religious freedom. The First Amendment now denies the right of government to enforce religion. The Statue of Liberty at the entrance to New York harbor remains a monument against Rome and against the history of religious persecution in Europe. In the United States, the state is separate from the church, and the church is separate from the state. Both have their place, and both are to remain free. Yet history reveals that Protestant America has never completely cut loose from the City of Seven Hills, from the Vatican itself.

On May 21, 1888, a New Hampshire Christian senator introduced the following bill into the fiftieth Congress, "Be it enacted by the Senate and the House of Representatives of the United States of America in Congress assembled, that no person, or corporation, or the agent, servant, or the employee of any person or corporation, shall perform or authorize to be performed any secular work . . . on the first day of the week, commonly known as the Lord's day" (*The National Sunday Law, Arguments of Alonzo T. Jones before the United States Senate Committee on Education and Labor at Washington, D.C., December 13, 1888.* 1889, p. v.). The purpose of this bill was to produce enforced Sunday keeping nationwide, and this proposed legislation had the support of Christian churches across America who were seeking to inject more religion into an increasingly secular society. Yet the Blair Sunday bill was finally ruled unconstitutional, and it died in committee.

That was over a hundred years ago. Yet the problem of immorality remains; in fact, it is getting worse. Every Christian knows society is in moral trouble, and we struggle for solutions. What does the future hold? Bible prophecy predicts that what happened in Europe leading to the forming of the beast will eventually happen in America leading to the image of the beast. In the fourth century, Rome was disintegrating. Constantine decided that the solution to the problem was to unite the government of Caesar with the Roman Catholic Church and to enforce the keeping of Sunday. Something similar will happen again. During a future crisis, in an hour of desperation, Protestant America will finally conclude that the only solution to the national emergency will be to unite the church with the federal government and to enforce the keeping of Sunday.

Pastor John Hagee, a much-respected Christian television evangelist, recently said, "I believe that in the next two years America will either return to God—or we will be a nation that goes beyond the brink and forever turns away from God. We are in that decision-making process now. It's time we rise up and Take America Back!" (John Hagee Ministries, *Ministry Resource Catalog*. Fall issue, 1999-2000, back cover). Pastor Hagee is correct when he says America needs to come back to God, yet (and I trust he would agree) this must be done through the love of Jesus Christ without the use of force.

On May 31, 1998, Pope John Paul II issued a lengthy pastoral letter, *Dies Domini* (The Day of the Lord), which contained a passionate appeal for the revival of Sunday observance. The pope said the prevailing neglect of Sunday reflects a spiritual crisis inside the Catholic Church and within Christianity in general. Notice his words: "The Lord's Day has structured the history of the Church through two thousand years: how could we think that it will not continue to shape the future?" Shockingly, the pope then urged world governments to enforce Sunday laws! "In the particular circumstances of our own time, Christians will naturally strive to ensure that civil legislation respects their duty to keep Sunday holy." Such statements are right in line with this official Vatican position: "Christians should seek recognition of Sundays and the Church's holy days as legal holidays" (*Catechism of the Catholic Church,* p. 528. 1994, italics supplied).

This view is shared by Pat Robertson, the founder of the Christian Coalition. In his best-selling book, *The New World Order,* Pat Robertson (like Pastor Hagee) correctly emphasizes the need for America to come back to God. His book envisions a time when this will occur. But he also writes: "The next obligation that a citizen of God's world order owes is to himself. 'Remember the Sabbath day, to keep it holy,' is a command for the personal benefit of each citizen. . . . Only when people are permitted to rest from their labors, to meditate on God, to consider His way, to dream of a better world can there be progress and genuine human betterment. . . . Laws in America that mandated a day of rest from incessant commerce have been nullified as a violation of the separation of church and state" (Pat Robertson, *The New World Order,* p. 236. 1991).

Do you realize what you just read? Pat Robertson is envisioning an America that has returned to God. As part of this new world order, he also sees an America that is keeping the Sabbath, yet by the Sabbath, he really means Sunday. He then looks back to the days of colonial America when Sunday was enforced by law. He wants to see this again. He says what is stopping Sunday laws from being enforced is the separation of church and state, which, he has concluded, is really a doctrine of the liberal left. This is a mistake. The founding fathers separated government and religion as a reaction to the Church of Rome and in favor of inalienable rights. As we have already seen, the Catholic Church is against the separation of church and state and is in favor of Sunday laws. When Protestants attack the separation of church and state and at the same time seek for Sunday laws, "They know not what they do." They are really lining up with the Roman Catholic Church and are preparing the way for the image of the beast and for the enforcement of his mark.

In the blazing light of Bible prophecy, these developments are more chilling than the scariest horror movie. I am not questioning anyone's sincerity or deciding people's destinies, yet the truth must be spoken. *Truth Left Behind* may never become as "wildly popular" as *Left Behind,* and it probably won't receive a host of positive reviews from Christian leaders nationwide. Nor will its contents be viewed as altogether politically correct. But, like Martin Luther, I have my orders, and they come from above. How many people accepted the preaching of Noah? How many boarded the ark? I am writing this book because the Spirit of God is compelling me and because Christians must be warned. Lucifer himself is hiding underneath many of Christianity's most popular trends. In fact, the enemy has recently spoken directly from heaven in support of Sunday observance. Have you heard of the apparitions of Mary? They are definitely increasing. We should have no doubt they really come from Satan. Notice these words from a Catholic author who has compiled an entire book about these appearances: "One evening our Lady appeared to a local farmer, Michael O'Donnel. She told him, 'Preserve Sunday for prayer' " (*The Thunder of Justice,* by Ted and Maureen Flynn, MaxKol Communications, Inc., 1993, p. 30).

"Those who fail to learn the lessons of history are condemned to repeat its mistakes." It already happened in Europe. The Roman Empire was falling apart, so Constantine decided to unite the government of Caesar with the Roman Catholic Church and to enforce the keeping of Sunday. This helped form the beast, and it will happen again in America. Our country is now sinking in the quicksand of sin, and immorality is raging out of control. Like the approaching footsteps of a midnight thief, the final crisis is coming. Prophecy predicts that in a soon-coming dramatic hour of desperation, America will reject over two hundred years of freedom. Sincere, and yet misguided Christians will take the reins of government. The appropriate separation of government and religion will disappear as Protestant America forms an image of the Roman Catholic Church. In a final attempt to bring America back to God, Sunday observance will once again be enforced by law. Yet this time, unlike the past, the enforcement will be universal. Protestants, Catholics, and even the apparitions of Mary, will all be united in this. The reasons will sound good; the movement will look Christian, and it will seem like our only hope. Yet deep in the midst of these turbulent waters will be Satan himself. He will have finally pulled off his ultimate masterpiece of delusion. He will have led Christians, in the name of the Lamb, to enforce the Mark of the Beast. Those who refuse to cooperate will not be able to buy or sell. And this is not an issue that some fictitious Tribulation Force will have to deal with. No. It will apply to you and me.

"He causeth all, both small and great, rich and poor, free and bond, to receive a mark in their right hand, or in their foreheads: And that no man might buy or sell, save he that had the mark, or the name of the beast, or the number of his name" (Revelation 13:16, 17). Notice carefully that people will get either the mark, the name, or the number. This doesn't mean the government will someday say, "Take your pick. Do you want the mark, the name, or the number?"—as is taught in *The Mark—The Beast Rules The World* (p. 86).

Not a chance. We are dealing here with deep spiritual issues. Sunday is the "mark" of Rome's authority. And just like "the name" of God refers to His character (Exodus 34:5-7), even so does "the name of the beast" refer to his character. The beast "thinks" it's OK to change God's law (Daniel 7:25). Those who think like this during the closing seconds of time will be sharing in the character of the beast. They will have his name on their foreheads, instead of the name of the heavenly Father (Revelation 14:1).

What about that mysterious "number of his name . . . 666" (Revelation 13:17, 18)? Consider this: What day was man created? On the sixth day. What day did God rest? On the seventh day (Genesis 1:26; 2:1-3). What number is God's number all throughout Revelation? Seven! The book of Revelation talks about seven churches (1:20), seven lampstands (1:20), seven stars (1:20), seven seals (5:1), seven trumpets (8:2), and finally seven last plagues (15:1), which will be emptied on those who get the number 666! Revelation says that 666 is man's number (Revelation 13:18), representing man trying to take the place of God. Seven is God's number, representing complete submission to Jesus Christ, our Creator. In fact, Jesus is represented in Revelation as a Lamb with "seven horns and seven eyes" (5:6), therefore the number seven is also Jesus Christ's special number. Those who keep the Sabbath reveal to the whole universe that they have entirely surrendered pride and self to the love of Jesus Christ, the Maker of all life, and to the full power of His cross. By God's grace, they overcome where Lucifer failed. *This is the core issue.*

When the Mark of the Beast is finally enforced by law around the world, the Good Shepherd will call His sheep. During that fateful crisis, there will be sincere Catholics and Protestants everywhere who have never understood the real issues. The Spirit of the Almighty will talk to their hearts. The three angels' messages will be heard from the pulpit, in print, on the radio, on television, on the World Wide Web, and via satellite. People will have a chance to learn what is truth. Jesus Christ will be lifted up, His cross will be seen, and actual cause of His death will be more deeply understood by Christians. Why did Jesus die? The Bible says, "Christ died for our sins" (1 Corinthians 15:3). What is sin? "Sin is the transgression of the law" (1 John 3:4). Simply put the pieces together. Jesus Christ died because human beings have broken the Ten Commandments, including the forgotten one, which says, "Remember the sabbath day, to keep it holy" (Exodus 20:8). Therefore Jesus Christ, our Creator, also died because we broke His Sabbath!

During the crisis surrounding the Mark of the Beast, it will be understood that Jesus is the Savior of the world and the Maker of all life. The Sabbath will be presented as a special day, which uniquely reveals Jesus Christ and His love for His own lost world. He is the Lord of the Sabbath (Matthew 12:8). People will then be brought face to face with the core issue that will ultimately decide their destiny. Will they worship Jesus Christ, the Creator, and keep the commandments of God? Or will they worship the beast and his image, and receive his mark? Humanity will have reached its final crossroads. Heaven's clock will have struck the midnight moment. The last hour of decision will have come. During those closing seconds, the seventh-day Sabbath will represent allegiance to Jesus Christ, the Maker of all life, while Sunday will represent allegiance to Rome.

Jesus said, "If you love me, keep my commandments" (John 14:15). The heart of the issue is love for Jesus Christ. Out of sincere appreciation for His grace and for the magnitude of His sacrifice for the sins of the whole world, Christ's true followers will fully take their stand on the Lord's side, no matter what the cost. The three angels' messages are clear: Those who accept the gospel, embrace the Lamb, worship the Creator, and keep the commandments, will not receive the Mark of the Beast. This is what the Bible says! The third angel describes God's final apocalyptic people in this way: "Here is the patience of the saints: here are they that keep the commandments of God, and the faith of Jesus" (Revelation 14:12).

During planet Earth's last crisis, when the Mark of the Beast is globally enforced by law, after a person truly sees the core issue and then chooses to believe in Rome's Sunday instead of the Bible Sabbath of Jesus Christ—then and only then, will God Almighty look into the inner recesses of his or her mind, and consider that person to have the mark in the forehead. Those who don't believe in Sunday keeping, yet who go along with it because of intense social and economic pressure to conform, will receive the mark in their right hand. Those who reject the use of force, who follow the Lamb, keeping the Sabbath no matter what the cost, will be revealing their supreme loyalty to the great Creator of heaven and earth. They have the name of God in their foreheads.

After everyone has made his final choice, the hinges of heaven's door will close forever. Jesus Christ will then make this final, tremendous announcement: "He that is unjust, let him be unjust still: and he which is filthy, let him be filthy still: and he that is righteous, let him be righteous still: and he that is holy, let him be holy still. And, behold, I come quickly; and my reward is with me, to give to every man according as his work shall be" (Revelation 22:11, 12). A mysterious voice will thunder from the heavenly temple, commanding the seven angels: "Go your ways, and pour out the vials of the wrath of God upon the earth. And the first went, and poured out his vial upon the earth; and there fell a noisome and grievous sore upon the men which had the mark of the beast, and upon them which worshipped his image" (Revelation 16:1, 2). These seven last plagues will totally desolate planet Earth. But as the Lord protected the Israelites in Egypt during the falling of the ten plagues (Exodus 8:22, 23; 9:6, 26; 10:21-23), even so will he fully protect His trusting and obedient children who have His holy name in their foreheads.

"He shall cover thee with his feathers, and under his wings shalt thou trust: his truth shall be thy shield and buckler. Thou shalt not be afraid for the terror by night; nor for the arrow that flieth by day; Nor for the pestilence that walketh in darkness; nor for the destruction that wasteth at noonday. A thousand shall fall at thy side, and ten thousand at thy right hand; but it shall not come nigh thee. Only with thine eyes shalt thou behold and see the reward of the wicked. Because thou hast made the LORD, which is my refuge, even the most High, thy habitation; There shall no evil befall thee , neither shall any plague come nigh thy dwelling" (Psalm 91:4-10).

At the conclusion of the seven last plagues, at the end of "the time of trouble such as never was," God's loyal people shall look up with wonder and see the coming of the King. "Then shall appear the sign of the Son of man in heaven: and then shall all the tribes of the earth mourn, and they shall see the Son of man coming in the clouds of heaven with power and great glory. And he shall send his angels with a great sound of a trumpet, and they shall gather together his elect from the four winds, from one end of heaven to the other" (Matthew 24:30, 31). Contrary to the fictitious account of *Left Behind*, this is when the Rapture takes place!

Jesus Christ, the Babe of Bethlehem, the carpenter's Son, the Good Shepherd, the Lamb of God, the King of kings, the Lord of the Sabbath, and the Maker of all life, the One who loves us and died for us, will soon return to take His children home. Oh friend, will we be "caught up" on that great day? Will we follow the Bible or tradition? True Protestantism or Jesuit futurism? The Creator or the beast? Will we be marked in our minds or will we have the name of God in our foreheads? The choice is up to us. It is up to you. "If any man have an ear, let him hear" (Revelation 13:9).

CHAPTER

The Flames of the Martyrs Still Speak

The gloves are off, and the battle is launched between the forces of good and evil for the very souls of men and women around the globe" (*The Mark—The Beast Rules The World,* inside cover). So begins book eight of the *Left Behind* novels. Tragically, this entire drama places the last end-time "battle between the forces of good and evil" only after the Rapture. This is also the teaching of Dr. John Walvoord, Hal Lindsey, Jack Van Impe, John Hagee, Peter and Paul Lalonde, Grant Jeffrey, and countless others. These are sincere Christians whom God is using, yet they have left behind some of the most serious Bible truths. Through their acceptance of Jesuit futurism, in contrast to the teachings of Martin Luther, John Calvin, John Wesley, and thousands of other historic Protestants, they do not realize who the real beast of Revelation is. Yet now our eyes have been opened. Now we know the truth. It will not be easy, but we must stand up for Jesus Christ, no matter what the cost.

As we near the end of this book, I want to focus on a lesson of faith and courage—of standing up for Jesus Christ. Turning away from *Left Behind* fiction with its future imaginary Antichrist, we are about to look at the very real story of a real man who did battle the beast. This battle took place in the 1400s, during the time of the famous Roman Catholic Council of Constance, in Constance, Germany. The council met November 1, 1414 and continued until April 22, 1418. "The total number of the clergy alone present at the council, though perhaps not all of them all the time, was four patriarchs, twenty-nine cardinals, thirty-three archbishops, one hundred and fifty bishops, one hundred and thirty-four abbots, two hundred and fifty doctors, and lesser clergy, amounting to eighteen thousand. With the emperor and his train, kings, dukes, lords, and other nobles, the members were ordinarily fifty thousand. At certain periods of the conference there were as many as one hundred thousand present. Thirty thousand horses were fed, and thirty thousand beds were provided by the city" (Alonzo T. Jones, *Ecclesiastical Empire,* Review and Herald Pub. Co. Battle Creek, Mich.: 1901, p. 553). In our modern terminology we would have said, "This is a big event. Parking is limited."

The Council of Constance condemned the writings of John Wycliffe of England, who lived in the 1300s. Wycliffe taught at Oxford University and has been called "The Morning Star of the Reformation." The movie, *John Wycliffe—The Morning Star,* was awarded the title of Best Film from the Christian Film Distributor's Association. Before Martin Luther, John Wycliffe protested against Rome, was the first to translate the Bible into English, taught salvation by faith in Jesus Christ, placed the Word of God above popes and kings, and openly declared papal Rome to be the great Antichrist of Scripture. The Council of Constance, more than forty years after Wycliffe's death, decreed that his decaying bones should be literally dug out of his grave and publicly burned. His ashes were triumphantly thrown into a nearby brook. "This brook," says an old writer, "hath conveyed his ashes into Avon, Avon into Severn, Severn into the narrow seas, they into the main ocean. And thus the ashes of Wycliffe are the emblems of his doctrine, which now is dispersed all the world over" (T. Fuller, *Church History of Britain,* b. 4, sec. 2, par. 54).

John Huss of Bohemia read the writings of John Wycliffe and continued many of his reforms. After denouncing John Wycliffe, the Council of Constance summoned John Huss, condemning him to the flames. Jerome of Prague was a good friend of Huss, and in April of 1415, before the martyrdom of Huss, Jerome arrived at Constance, hoping to help his friend. Unfortunately, he was seized by friends of the pope, cruelly dragged through the streets in chains, and promptly thrown into a dark, miserable, rat-infested dungeon. For almost a year, he was transferred from dungeon to dungeon. At last he was brought before the council. Before that vast assembly these false charges were read against him: "1. He was a derider of the papal dignity. 2. An opposer of the pope. 3. An enemy to the cardinals. 4. A persecutor of the prelates. 5. A hater of the Christian religion" (*Fox's Book of Martyrs,* Zondervan Pub. House: Grand Rapids, Mich.: 1926, p. 145). Jerome was then commanded to accept the Catholic faith or be burned at the stake.

Weakened by almost a year of horrible treatment, Jerome's faith wavered, and he agreed in some measure to submit to Rome. But after he was returned to his rat-infested cell, he saw more clearly what he had done. He thought about his friend John Huss, who had died in the flames. He thought about his Savior, whom he had pledged to serve, who for his sake had endured the unspeakable nightmare of the cross. Before his decision to compromise he had found comfort amid all his sufferings in the assurance of God's favor; but now remorse and doubts tortured his soul. He knew that still other compromises must be made before he would be released, which could only end in his complete apostasy from the Bible and from what he now knew to be right. As he looked into the whiskered faces of those rats and felt cockroaches crawling around his toes, Jerome made his decision. He would no longer deny Jesus Christ.

Soon Jerome was brought again before the council, but now he was determined to boldly confess his faith and to follow his friend John Huss to the flames. He publicly renounced his former denial, and demanded, as a dying man, an opportunity to make his defense. "You have held me shut up three hundred and forty days in a frightful prison," he said, "in the midst of filth, noisomeness, stench, and the utmost want of everything; you then bring me out before you, and lending an ear to my mortal enemies, you refuse to hear me. . . . If you be really wise men and the lights of the world, take care not to sin against justice. As for me, I am only a feeble mortal; my life is but of little importance" (Bonnechose, *The Reformers Before the Reformation,* vol. 2, pp. 146, 147). His request was finally granted. In the presence of many judges, priests, and nobles of Europe, Jerome knelt down and prayed for the Holy Spirit to take over.

Jerome then gave an absolutely sizzling defense in behalf of the truth. Referring to John Huss, he declared, "I knew him from his childhood. He was a most excellent man, just and holy; he was condemned, notwithstanding his innocence. . . . I also am ready to die. I will not recoil before the torments that are prepared for me by my enemies and false witnesses, who will one day have to render an account of their impostures before the great God, whom nothing can deceive. . . . Of all the sins that I have committed since my youth, none weigh so heavily on my mind, and cause me such remorse, as that which I committed in this fatal place, when I approved of the iniquitous sentence rendered against Wycliffe, and against the holy martyr, John Huss, my master and my friend. Yes! I confess it from my heart, and declare with horror that I disgracefully quailed when, through a dread of death, I condemned their doctrines. I therefore supplicate . . . Almighty God to pardon me my sins, and this one in particular, the most heinous of all." Pointing his finger at his judges, he declared, "You condemned Wycliffe and John Huss. . . . The things which they affirmed, and which are irrefutable, I also think and declare, like them" (Ibid.).

His hearers were stunned! "Shut him up!" cried his enemies. "What need have we of further proof? We behold with our own eyes the most obstinate of heretics!" Yet Jerome stood unmoved, like a mighty rock amidst a hurricane. He then thundered back, "What! do you suppose I fear to die? You have held me in a frightful dungeon, more horrible than death itself. You have treated me more cruelly than a Turk, Jew, or pagan, and my flesh has literally rotted off my bones alive, and yet I make no complaint, for lamentation ill becomes a man of heart and spirit; but I cannot but express my astonishment at such great barbarity toward a Christian" (Ibid., pp. 151-153). He was then grabbed by his guards and hurried back to the rats and cockroaches.

He was soon visited in his cell and given one last opportunity to return to Rome. Jerome responded, "Prove to me from the Holy Writings that I am in error!" "The Holy Writings!" said one of his tempters, "is everything to be judged by them? Who can understand them until the church has interpreted them?" Jerome replied, "Are the traditions of men more worthy of faith than the gospel of our Savior?" "Heretic!" was the response, "I repent having pleaded so long with you. I see that you are urged on by the devil" (J. A. Wylie, *The History of Protestantism*, b. 3, ch. 10). Thus Jerome, even though he was accused of being inspired by Satan, refused to bow down to the traditions of mere mortals. "The Bible and the Bible only," was his motto. There is a lesson for us in this. We may also be accused of being Lucifer-led when we turn away from human traditions, popular ideas, and common practices. Nevertheless, we should stick to "the Holy Writings," no matter what the cost.

Finally sentence was passed, and Jerome was led out to the very same spot were John Huss had yielded up his life. He went singing on his way, his face lighted up with joy and peace. His gaze was fixed upon Jesus Christ, the Maker of all life, so why should he fear death? Upon arriving at the place, Jerome once more knelt down to say a heart-felt prayer. He was then tied to a stake, and branches of wood were piled around his feet. When the executioner stepped up to light the fire, this holy martyr exclaimed, "Come forward boldly; apply the fire before my face. Had I been afraid, I should not be here." As the flames began to rise, Jerome prayed again. His last words were, "Lord, Almighty Father . . . have pity on me, and pardon me my sins; for Thou knowest that I have always loved Thy truth" (Bonnechose, vol. 2, p. 168).

Do we love the truth above tradition? Are we willing to stand for Jesus Christ, the Maker of all life, and for the Bible, no matter what it cost? Friend, Jesus loves each of us personally. He loves you. He has a special place in His heart for you and your family. He gave Jerome the strength to stand up for what he knew to be right, and He will do the same for you. Yes, He will even give you the courage to follow the three angels' messages! As we trust God for forgiveness through the blood of the Lamb, let's determine right now to be among that final people of whom it is written, "Here is the patience of the saints: here are they that keep the commandments of God, and the faith of Jesus" (Revelation 14:12). Those who do this will be the Jeromes of the last generation. They will be ready for the coming of Jesus Christ on a pure white cloud to take His children home (Revelation 14:14-16).

CHAPTER

New Babylon and the Shepherd's Call

In the *Left Behind* novels, "His Excellency Global Community Potentate Nicolae Carpathia" transfers his U.N. headquarters to ancient Babylon in modern Iraq, renaming it New Babylon. From this new center, fully equipped with the latest in high-tech intelligence devices, Carpathia monitors world affairs. A highly trained New World Order Police Force carry out the will of their leader, seeking to discover all opposition to his plans. But in spite of the Global Community's massively coordinated efforts, the Tribulation Force of secret believers often evade detection, maintaining their loyalty to Jesus Christ. Some even work in disguise for Carpathia himself. In book number eight, "The Trib Force moles inside the palace of New Babylon face tragedy and danger, and they must flee, take the mark, or suffer the consequences" (*The Mark—The Beast Rules The World,* inside cover). This thrilling and action-packed story is *Left Behind*'s version of how prophecies about Babylon in the book of Revelation might be fulfilled at the end of time.

In spite of the sincerity of this perspective, once again, there is something wrong with this picture. By now you should be able to discern the inherent futurism and mistaken literalism of this wildly popular story. Sadly, *Left Behind* is not only dealing with fictitious people, but also with fictitious theology. For hundreds of years Protestant scholars did not apply Revelation's prophecy about Babylon to any literal city in modern Iraq at all. A closer look at the facts will reveal the absolute necessity of an entirely different interpretation from that of *Left Behind*. Revelation 17 describes Babylon as "the great whore" (17:1); "decked with gold" (17:4); "arrayed in purple and scarlet" (17:4); with "a golden cup" (17:4); "THE MOTHER OF HARLOTS" (17:5); "drunken with the blood of the saints" (17:6); sitting upon "seven mountains" (17:9); who reigns over "the kings of the earth" (17:18). Does this sound like Carpathia's New Babylon? The fact is, a woman in Bible prophecy represents a church. Of the bride of Christ we read, "His wife hath made herself ready" (Revelation 19:7). Paul also wrote, "Christ also loved the church, and gave himself for it" (Ephesians 5:25). Paul longed to present the church as "a chaste virgin to Christ" (2 Corinthians 11:2). A chaste (pure) woman represents God's church. Therefore, the great whore in Revelation 17 must represent an apostate church, which has fallen away from the truth.

During the Persian Gulf war in 1991, after Saddam Hussein announced his plans to rebuild the literal city of Babylon in Iraq, books on Bible prophecy began to flow from Christian presses teaching that this development was one of the major omens of the last days. Zondervan quickly issued an updated version of John F. Walvoord's bestseller, *Armageddon, Oil and the Middle East Crisis.* The initial print order was for one million copies, nine of which were reportedly ordered by the White House. Yet interestingly enough, at the same time, *Time* magazine ran an essay called "Apocalypse Now?" Amazingly, it insightfully declared that the current trend toward identifying modern Iraq with the Babylon of Revelation, "somewhat awkwardly . . . undercuts a long standing Protestant tradition that this symbol of corruption refers to the church of Rome" (*Time,* Feb. 11, 1991, p. 88). Stunning! *Time* magazine was far more accurate than *Left Behind.*

There is only one church in history that fits every tiny detail of Revelation 17. It is the Church of Rome. Rome is famous as "the city of seven hills." Purple and scarlet are the official colors of the Catholic cardinals. The Roman Church is the richest church in the world. It has been said that there is more gold in the Vatican than in all of Fort Knox. A golden cup is used by the pope in St. Peter's Cathedral during the high mass. Historically, the Roman Church has drunk deeply of the blood of the martyrs, being responsible for the deaths of 50 to 100 million so-called "heretics" such as John Huss and Jerome. Papal Rome specifically refers to herself as "The Mother Church." And this is the only church that has ever "ruled over kings." Thus, every piece fits perfectly.

The second of God's "Three Angels' Messages Force" is now crying out, saying, "Babylon is fallen, is fallen, that great city, because she made all nations drink of the wine of the wrath of her fornication" (Revelation 14:8). Notice that Babylon has "fallen." This means she originally stood tall, but she has fallen from grace. She is now making all the earth drunk with her wine. Wine in the Bible is used to represent teachings or doctrines. The pure doctrine of Jesus Christ is called "new wine" (Matthew 9:17). The wine of Babylon represents the false teachings of "The Mother Church," which now circle the globe. The nations are "drunk," which means they are confused. In fact, the very word *Babylon* literally means "confusion," pointing back to the Tower of Babel when God confused the languages of its rebellious builders (Genesis 11).

The scarlet lady of the Apocalypse is called, "MYSTERY, BABYLON THE GREAT, THE

MOTHER OF HARLOTS" (Revelation 17:5). Now look carefully. Notice that papal Rome is referred to as a "MOTHER OF HARLOTS." This means she is not the only harlot. She has harlot daughters. If the mother represents the Roman Catholic Church, then who are her daughters? Would not the daughters represent churches that have come out of her somewhat, yet who actually continue to follow her teachings? The Protestant churches did come out of Catholicism in the Reformation, yet did they come fully out? They took Sunday with them. But in those early "times of this ignorance God winked at" many things (Acts 17:30). The Protestant Reformers were just coming out of the midnight blackness of the Dark Ages. But we are in the time of the end when knowledge is increasing (Daniel 12:4). It is now time for God's "Three Angels' Messages Force" to make it plain so that Christians everywhere will understand the truth about the beast, the image, and the mark (Revelation 14:9).

Yet during these closing seconds of history, what are many Protestant churches doing? They are teaching the false prophecies of Jesuit futurism about a one-man Antichrist who is not even here yet. As we have seen, this is a Roman Catholic doctrine. Is it possible? Could this make these churches daughters of the mother? The second angel cries out, "Babylon is fallen, is fallen" (Revelation 14:8). Notice the word *fallen* is mentioned twice. This reveals that both the mother and the daughters have fallen from grace. Thus, the word *Babylon* applies to them both. It is a family name.

Yet there is something very important we need to understand. There are true Christians inside both the mother and the daughters. How do we know this? For one thing, if we simply look around, it's obvious. Second, the Bible says, "I heard another voice from heaven, saying, Come out of her, my people" (Revelation 18:4). Inside both the Catholic Church and the Protestant churches of today, God has His people. In this book I have talked about Christian leaders who are now influencing hundreds of thousands of people. I have even gone so far as to mention names such as Dr. John Walvoord, Hal Lindsey, Jack Van Impe, Peter and Paul Lalonde, John Hagee, and Grant Jeffrey. This entire book is a critique of the work of Tim LaHaye and Jerry Jenkins, the authors of the *Left Behind* novels, which Barnes and Noble voted to be the "best-selling series of all time." Thus, I am talking about very well-known Christians. I am using their names not to condemn them personally, but only as examples, for there are countless others who teach similar ideas. I believe these men and their ministries are committed to Jesus Christ and are truly seeking to advance the cause of the kingdom. I also believe God is using them in many ways, just like the Father spoke through Peter when he confessed his firm faith in Christ (Matthew 16:15-17).

Yet I cannot avoid the fact that, in the light of

Scripture, prophecy, and Protestant history, error has entered these ministries. The very doctrine of the Antichrist is now being taught. Jesus also said to Peter, " 'Get behind Me, Satan!' " (Matthew 16:23, NKJV), because the devil was secretly at work. This is what I call the "Peter Principle." Consider this: Peter was one of the original disciples, and he was also the very one the Holy Spirit used so mightily on the Day of Pentecost (Acts 2). Yet, in the above instance, Satan entered Peter without his even knowing it! Can this happen again? Can it happen to sincere Christians today who are even leading major ministries? Yes it can, and it is!

At this very moment, false prophecy is flowing like a tidal wave through Christianity. Now listen. There really is a mother with her daughters described in Revelation. This idea does not come from Steve Wohlberg. And there really are a whole lot of genuine Christians, who, without knowing it are inside both of them. To deny this, is to deny the Bible! Yet God is now flashing at us all a blaze of new light. In "the time of the end . . . knowledge shall be increased" (Daniel 12:4). Jesus Christ Himself is now practically thundering from heaven, saying, "Come out of her, my people" (Revelation 18:4). Will we listen to His voice?

Three shepherds with large flocks of sheep once came upon the same water hole. Their sheep became all mixed up with each other, yet the shepherds were not concerned. They sat on a rock, ate lunch, and talked away the hours. Late in the afternoon, they said "Goodbye," and then walked in opposite directions. What about the sheep? How could they tell them apart? How could this mixed-up group ever be properly separated? Then each shepherd gave his own distinct whistle, and as that special sound entered into the ears and brains of each sheep, each individual animal heard the call. Each knew his master's voice and followed him.

In these last days, the Good Shepherd is calling His sheep. At this very moment, Jesus Christ sees millions of His children all mixed up and confused inside the mother and the daughters. The Prince of Peace declares, "Other sheep I have, which are not of this fold: them also I must bring, and they shall hear my voice; and there shall be one fold, and one shepherd" (John 10:16). Did you catch that? This tells us that Jesus' ultimate plan is to have only one flock with one Shepherd! Do we hear His voice? At this very moment, the Almighty God is calling us out of all Babylonian confusion, out of all false doctrine, away from Jesuit futurism, and into the blazing light of end-time Bible truth.

The Reformation is not yet over! The same Holy Spirit who moved upon Martin Luther in the 1500s is now compelling Christians in the twenty-first century to give the three angels' messages. Those three angels represent a movement of truth, centered in Jesus Christ, right before the end. In contrast to *Left Behind*'s fictitious "Tribulation Force," God's real "Three Angels' Messages Force" is here now, and it is daily growing in power. More and more people around the world are hearing and responding to these super-clarifying, life-changing messages. They are now being proclaimed with a loud voice from the pulpit, in print, on the radio, on television, via satellite, and on the World Wide Web. And through the pages of this little book, they are now being heard by you!

Satan would love to aim a SCUD missile and shoot these messages right out of the sky! But he can't. They are unstoppable! Why? Because Jesus Christ Himself is behind them. The three angels' messages are part of "the Revelation of Jesus Christ" (Revelation 1:1), therefore they come from Him. Soon "the earth [will be] lightened with his glory" (Revelation 18:1) and the last call will be given (Revelation 18:4). The United States federal government has adopted the slogan, "Uncle Sam Wants You." The truth is, "King Jesus Christ Wants You" to join God's real "Three Angels' Messages Force." The last chapter of the Bible says, "I, Jesus, have sent mine angel to testify unto you these things in the churches" (Revelation 22:16). The God of the universe is now searching for more than a few good men.

It is not an accident you have read this book. The Almighty is now calling us to come all the way out of Babylon, to keep all of the Ten Commandments, including the forgotten fourth, and to trust fully in the love, mercy, and grace of Jesus Christ. That's what the Bible says! Inexhaustible and outrageous love speaks from the Cross, saying, "Believe, and follow Me." By God's grace, let's be the Jeromes of this final generation, finishing the Reformation.

It is time to recover all truth left behind.

Additional Resources
(with Steve Wohlberg)

Truth Left Behind

- A video series based on this book.
- Available as an audio album.

The Left Behind Deception

- A smaller book containing the first three chapters of *Truth Left Behind.*
- Available in large quantities. Great for sharing!

Israel in Prophecy

- A 10-part video series about Israel, Jerusalem, the Temple, and Armageddon.
- Available in an audio album.
- *Exploding the Israel Deception* (companion sharing book).

Amazing Discoveries Bible Prophecy Seminar

- A major 24-part series about Earth's final days.
- Available on video or in an audio album.

Jewish Discoveries in Scripture

- An 8-part video series where Messianic Jews discuss the Torah (the first five books of the Bible), the Ten Commandments, and the Messiah. Great for sharing with your Jewish friends.

To order:
Call Amazing Discoveries: (800) 795-7171
(Visa / MasterCard accepted)

Or write:
Texas Media Center
P.O. Box 330489
Fort Worth, Texas 76163

www.truthleftbehind.com